NO

G000047796

MATTER

WHERE

ABI

SHAW

ISBN:

(Paperback) 978-1-916529-03-8

(ebook) 978-1-916529-04-5

Cover design by. Tom Sulley

The Unbound Press

www.theunboundpress.com

Hey unbound one!

Welcome to this magical book brought to you by The Unbound Press.

At The Unbound Press we believe that when women write freely from the fullest expression of who they are, it can't help but activate a feeling of deep connection and transformation in others. When we come together, we become more and we're changing the world, one book at a time!

This book has been carefully crafted by both the author and publisher with the intention of inspiring you to move ever more deeply into who you truly are.

We hope that this book helps you to connect with your Unbound Self and that you feel called to pass it on to others who want to live a more fully expressed life.

With much love,

Nicola Humber

Founder of The Unbound Press

www.theunboundpress.com

The answer is always love.

This book is dedicated to my two babies, who remind me all too often, in subtle ways, that I need to get a proper job! They are my proper job but still, this feeling of momentary inadequacy has fuelled me to finish this tale so thank you. 'You are my world.' When I was writing this dedication in Java, my daughter came over to me and asked me what I was doing. It's like she knew my focus was on her. That girl was born with her third eye well and truly wide open, an indigo child and boy, does she know me best in this world. My boy, my love, you can now finally tell people that your Mum is a writer, if you want to.

To my darling Belfast bestie, who has heard all these stories first-hand and kept me laughing through the highs and the lows. You are my inspiration to just crack on and get it done. Life has thrown you so many challenges, yet your humour remains intact, and your commitment to your family is exceptional. You are the human embodiment of an angel.

Finally, my Fairy Godmother, my councillor, without whom I may not be here today. I certainly wouldn't be the woman I am. You literally saved my life. How can I ever say thank you enough? I made you a promise and I could never break it. Here is my tale … finally!

Endorsements

"A tale of adventure, strength and lightness, as Abi navigates the ups and downs of life with humour and honesty. Created to inspire, challenge and move us into living a life full of possibilities. "

Poppy Delbridge, Best-selling Author, Wellness Educator
and Founder of Rapid Tapping ®

"Abi Shaw is brilliant. Every page of this book - and her life - invites you to keep turning. Be ready to wrap yourself up in her "warm, soothing blanket of truth."

Cortney McDermott, bestselling author of *Change Starts Within You*
and *Give Yourself Permission*

"Beautiful sparks of magic and wisdom dance and leap from every line of Abi's timeless storytelling. Stories of love told with sage like truth. Within Abi's words are lessons on life, loss, forgiveness, reclamation and honesty that travel across oceans on a journey of connection to one's true self."

Kate Taylor, Life Design & Business Empowerment Coach

"It's really, well - real! Which in itself is incredibly refreshing."

Pete Hunt, Founder & CEO theprivilegedman.com

Author Bio

Abi Shaw is an eternal optimist. She is first and foremost a mother to her two mini-adventurers. As a trio, they have ventured from the Midlands to the Côte D'Azur, from Cornwall to Bali – building their home from love and laughter instead of bricks and mortar. Her love of people and appetite for life have remained constant through the inevitable changing tides of life. As a passionate woman, 'to settle' is not an infinitive she prescribes to and so welcomes the surprises this predictably invites. Although pragmatic, she ensures these new chapters always have hints of elegance and glamour. Even in the most challenging of times.

As the wise ones say, pain is inevitable, suffering is optional. 'To love' is her infinitive. 'To love' is Abi Shaw.

The Biggest Thank You!

To all the wise and brilliant goddesses at The Unbound Press who supported me on this incredibly stimulating, fulfilling and emotional adventure.

To my beautiful girl for being the first person to read my memoir – you are brave like your Mum.

To my beautiful boy for your unwavering determination that inspires me every day.

To the cool genius, Tom Sulley, who gave my book the perfect face and to the pure joy who is Lynda Mangoro for giving my book the perfect body.

To my brainstorm buddy, Julie Buchanan, I promise to stop bombarding you now!

To Twyla Doone for your wordsmith magic and for giving me faith in the future of our planet.

To all my 'lovelies' who have offered me words of encouragement to get my spiel onto paper. As they say…it takes a village!

My Secret Garden

This isn't a self-help book. It's not an ode to myself and how well I've done through a serious blot on the landscape, so to speak. It's simply a tale about me, cancer, a beloved husband who became an even more beloved ex-husband, two children, many lovers and a humongous adventure. It's a fairground ride of highs and lows, stomach-wrenching moments of excruciating heartbreak and goosebump-inducing moments of joyous love, passion and thrills. I hope it makes you smile. I hope it makes you cringe. I hope it brings you tears, and above all, I hope it brings you hope if that's what you need. It's the ultimate of clichés, but every cloud does have a silver lining, and sometimes you need to be broken for the light to shine through. As my all-time favourite saying goes, 'Until you spread your wings, you have no idea how far you can fly.' From the Midlands to France, then Bali, back to France … for now. Who'd have thought it? Welcome to my secret garden.

My intention is not to place blame or shame. None of us are perfect and I most definitely include myself in that statement. How incredibly bland would the world be if we were? We are all simply doing our best. This is my truth, these are my memories, my feelings, my experiences, and I totally understand that it was a different experience for others involved. I mean no harm with any of the words I write, I truly mean that, but I simply cannot write about the silver lining without first explaining the cloud. I feel vulnerable sharing my story and I'm not sure if it makes me feel brave or cowardly, but what I do know for sure is that any feelings, extreme or subtle, are what I love, what I crave, and I do not shy away from them. Let's do this!

You will notice that this book is a compilation of stories, emails, suggestions, writing prompts, quotes, recipes and photos. I am a typical Libran who loves beautiful things. Whilst writing this book in Bali, I started posting my favourite photos on Instagram, so it seems only fitting that I include some of them in this book. For many years now, I have also sent a group email, firstly to promote my teeny-weeny tea business in France, and then it developed into more of a diary of 'musings from afar', so I have included some of these emails too. They are dear to me and reveal a lot. I hope you enjoy the ride as much as I have, and I hope you have a laugh because laughter really is the best medicine.

With all my love to the moon and back xxx

Who Am I?

Here's a bit about me. A first writing prompt from the book *Write On* by an incredible author, Qoya* sister and friend, Betsy Blankenbaker Murphy, allowed me to write about myself in a way I could never have done. Being asked if I identify with the sun or the moon was like a mirror being held up in front of my eyes and deep diving into my soul.

Tell why you are like the sun or the moon.

I feel like the moon rather than the sun. I'm not a big shining, 'you can't take your eyes off me' kind of light. But I am a source of light, wise light, subtle but very present and essential at times. A guiding light. I am more sultry than smoking hot. I am an observer, like the man on the moon. I'm happy to sit and listen and rarely make a bold statement for fear of saying something stupid, although I have learnt to ask questions. I guess I'm a half-moon. Yin and yang. The mother and the lover. The angel and the devil. The healthy and the extravagant. The homebody and the traveller. Happy in a beach hut and joyful in a luxury hotel. Relaxed in a Bali tie-dye dress and delighted in diamonds. I'm a chameleon and can change my look and demeanour accordingly and with very little effort. Something I actually enjoy. I can talk to almost anyone, but as I said, I would rather listen. I'm curious and driven yet sometimes lazy. Passionate yet calm. There is a mysteriousness, an unknown, about the moon which I have. I think people are often surprised by my not-so-innocent side. There is an old wisdom that I possess, especially when it comes to mothering. I am extremely feminine like the moon, rather than the sun who seems masculine to me. I am also understanding. I try to listen and not judge. I try not to

---

*Qoya is a movement system that I practise and through which I have met many incredible women. It is based on the idea that through movement, we remember. We remember our essence is wise, wild and free.

solve all the problems I hear about but rather accept them and not carry around bad feelings and take them too personally. Sometimes I am very present, like the full moon, and other times, you can barely see me, like a new moon, when I need my privacy and quiet time ... resting in my room on my own, which I always make into a beautiful haven. I am intrigued by the moon and follow its cycles. It affects everything we do as humans, more than we realise, I'm sure. 'Guarda la luna' (look at the moon) is something I say often to my kids. It's mesmerising and beautiful. It can charge crystals. It can charge water. It governs the tides of the powerful ocean that we have learnt to respect so much. It rules me. Now I'm not saying that I have such immense power, but with age, I have become more aware of my impact in this world and less meek and mild about that. Yes, I identify with the moon, just call me Mother Moon.

'Good sense of humour, dirty mind and beautiful heart. Deadly combination.'

– @fuckology, Instagram

'Wise but inquisitive, wild but cultivated and free
but with an understanding of what it is
to feel grounded.'

– By me about me

WARDROBE MAN AND ME

I was brought up to be independent and, apparently, I have my maternal poppa's stubbornness. I like to call it 'drive'! My parents were both teachers. I got through university with a first and oral distinction (which always makes me giggle), paid back my overdraft, and started working in PR and marketing. I was self-sufficient. I bought my first house with the second true love of my life and worked in marketing five days a week and on Saturdays in an interiors shop, buying, selling, merchandising, and proving my worth to this all-new, funky interior design company which offered me a full-time job within a matter of months.

Then I met my ex-husband. I was going about my daily work when a young, handsome and extremely confident man came into the shop. His parents were good clients already, and he'd been sent in to order wardrobes for his bedroom as he'd recently moved home. I don't remember giving him a second glance. He was just an extremely easy customer, and within half an hour, I had sold him a few thousand pounds worth of wardrobes and off he pottered. Job done. Nice one.

A few months later, and after a painful split from the man with whom I bought my first house, I went clubbing one night with my best friend. I was pretty merry, which means I get really chatty. As I walked down the stairs to the dance floor, I spotted 'wardrobe man' at the bar with a group of rather dashing friends. I made a beeline for him, pinned him in the corner and chatted his hind legs off. The chemistry was instant, and soon we were huddled together on the pavement outside the club, waiting for a cab back to mine. Now my beloved friend had hooked up with one of his friends, and I'm still not certain to this day as to how, but they ended up canoodling in my double bed, which left me and future-husband to create a makeshift love nest in the spare room with a few pillows, cushions and blankets. A rather humble start to what was to become a very glamorous life. My ex-husband was a professional sportsman, and within the year, we moved to Monaco. By the following year, we were married. That boy didn't mess about. Actually, that statement is rather ironic, as that boy did mess about and therein lay the tragedy.

The first wedding (we got married twice, as you do!) was in England. A quintessentially English 'country do' at the village church with a marquee on my brand-new parents-in-law's back lawn. I spent the day meeting and greeting an endless stream of my new husband's family, who I'd never met before. I wondered if he even knew who they all were. Then I danced my arse off with bottles of champagne in hand. I woke up in a seriously posh hotel with an almighty hangover but sadly without any appropriate clothing, so I enjoyed my maiden brekkie as a married woman dressed in black Nike joggers, a sheer mauve and sequined vest top and my gold Jimmy Choo wedding sandals, a sight I'm not sure the hotel manager had ever seen before.

The second wedding, one week later, was a delectably glitzy party in Monaco with all of our best friends. I got to wear my beautiful Spanish lace wedding dress again, along with the botanical gardens in my hair! We ate incredible food, danced the night away, then slipped off to St Tropez for a few nights of pure heaven by the beach. I was utterly besotted and deeply in love with my new husband.

Life in Monaco was hedonistic. We lived in a stunning apartment on the Grand Prix hairpin bend right in the centre of Monte Carlo. I had an incredible job working in the superyacht industry. I went to the gym with Shirly Bassey. My ex-husband was off competing around Europe most weekends where I'd join him, and the rest of the time, we partied hard ... Monaco, Nice, Cannes, Saint Tropez, Portofino. We spent time on yachts, at beach clubs and in exclusive hotels. In so many ways, we were living the dream.

THAT SINKING FEELING

To cut a long story short, we moved back to England when my ex stopped his sports career. I found it hard to leave my job and friends, but it wasn't long until we had two beautiful children and my life felt complete. I was blissfully happy and adored being a mummy, but as any parent knows, your life changes. I was in a dichotomy, blissfully happy as a new mum but trying to plaster over more and more cracks that were appearing in my love life.

My ex-husband had always been a drinker. Sadly, one drink just wasn't an option. It was always a slippery slope into a world of oblivion, hiding from his demons. In the early days, it wasn't a problem for me. I partied with him. We had time to recover. I had time to pick up the pieces and sweep the embarrassment and sadness under the carpet. He had time to pull himself out of his post-drinking blues. However, with babies on board, the stress of these episodes increased. I think he struggled with the normalcy of parenthood and married life. He was no longer my centre of attention. I now had three incredibly important people to look after besides myself.

When my son was only a couple of months old, we moved back to France on New Year's Eve, where my heart belonged. I remember sitting in the Euro Tunnel and feeding our tiny innocent baby, the car packed to the max with our life's belongings. I was so hopeful for a calmer life with less drinking.

We renovated the most beautiful 1920s villa in a picturesque Côte d'Azur village. This joint passion brought us really close. My ex-husband had a real gift for project management, and we both adore design. We were realising a huge dream and not far from moving into our perfect family home when disaster struck. We found out our builders (and best friends) were dishonest. Actually, let's not beat about the bush – they were professional crooks and had stolen a vast sum of money from us. It crucified my ex-husband. I lost a great friend (the builder's wife). Even our kids were great pals. The level of deceit still turns my stomach. I remember my hands physically shaking one day when we were about to confront them. This was the first real stress I had ever experienced in my life, and I believe it triggered what happened next. In fact, I'm sure of it.

I discovered a small insignificant mole on my back that I hadn't felt before. My doctor told me it was 'nothing to worry about' but suggested I see a dermatologist anyway. Thank goodness I did, as I was promptly diagnosed with a *level four ulcerated melanoma*. Still to this day, I have never googled those four words and I never ever will, but the reaction from the doctors made it very clear that this could be it. For a moment, my world stopped spinning.

For the first time ever, I had to put myself near the top of the list. I just didn't have the capacity to look after my ex-husband, my children and myself. I went inwards, the only place I knew to go that I could trust one hundred percent. I went quiet. Looking back, maybe he felt abandoned. I could no longer scoop him up from his post-drinking downers. My heart was already breaking. The sad realisation was dawning on me that the man I loved most in this world could not look after me when I needed him most. He was slowly checking out. He was falling out of love with me, with France, and was spending more and more time in London. His way of escaping the demons.

IF YOU WANT TO BE STRONG, LEARN HOW TO FIGHT ALONE

I cannot write this book without talking more about my cancer. I could hardly bring myself to write the next eight words, but, it really did change me for the better. It kept my anger and sadness from totally devouring me. What anger and sadness, you might ask? So if I thought things were pretty crappy at that point in my life, little did I know what was still to come …

I decided to follow my treatment in London at the Royal Marsden Hospital, a most remarkable place. I thought it would be easier for my ex-husband to be in England as he doesn't speak much French. Ironically he only ever came to one appointment with my specialist. Then I went solo. No words. I was then put on a trial that the hospital was conducting for melanoma patients. My lymph nodes were ultrasounded more or less every three months to check for any inflammation, a sign that the cancer might be spreading.

The frequent trips to hospital were a stressful yet weirdly reassuring ritual for five long years. I always wore the most inappropriate underwear for the check-ups with my wonderfully conventional specialist, who was constantly curious about my latest health 'fad', as he called them. He'd then tell me that if he'd been given my diagnosis, he would be eating all the red meat available to him and drinking red wine galore. But I felt safe in his hands, which is exactly what I needed as my ex-husband's hands, it turns out, were elsewhere.

A second writing prompt from the book *Write On* allowed me to reflect further on my cancer.

Tell about an ending in your life that really was a beginning.

My cancer. It's a cliché, but a thing needs to be broken before the light can shine through. My hideous cancer diagnosis turned my world upside down. It turned my husband away from me. It turned the volume of my love for my children to eardrum-bursting proportions. I can remember coming home from one doctor who had suggested I get some sleeping tablets and antidepressants, sitting in the hallway under the stairs, hiding away from my kids and sobbing with pure fear. I was scared shitless. I whispered to my ex-husband, 'Am I going to die?'. I don't remember his reaction or answer. In fact, I don't think he had one, and I knew then that I was going to be alone in this battle. He could barely look after himself, let alone his wife.

Chemotherapy and radiotherapy are not options for melanoma as they do not improve your chances, so the only 'treatment' I received was surgery to remove a large 10cm junk of flesh around my mole on Valentine's Day. The one romantic gesture I received was a rose from the hotel where we stayed the night before. My ex-husband left me in the hospital on the day of my surgery to fly back to France. Years later, I found out that he went on a massive bender that night, his way of blocking out reality, and I don't really blame him. The future looked bleak. It was his mother who helped me to convalesce, and I will always be grateful to her for that week.

Luckily, my incredible children were my saving grace. The week I was away for surgery, my son wet himself during his nap at school every single day. The day I got home, he stopped. Never underestimate the need they have for you. Before I left for surgery, I stuck a magical tree mural up on my daughter's wall with her. We lay under it and I told her that if she looked at the tree, she would always see me. Those feelings of immense, overwhelming love are still alive in me today, but the ghastly fear of not being around to see my kids grow up has totally evaporated. I made a decision not to find out the statistics for my survival rate. I didn't want to be put on a graph. I turned vegan and 80% raw (not for long, I might add). I concentrated on myself for the first time ever in my life. I had to withdraw into my inner soul to be able to cope, and in hindsight, that's maybe why my ex-husband wandered. It was the end of me as a person who had never been touched by cancer, but it was the beginning of me taking control of my life and how I live it. I signed up for retreats. I found my spiritual tribe. I got to bring my kids up my way. I chose which friends I trusted. I started living the richest life in all my glory, as a mother and a lover, as a daughter and a granddaughter, as a sister and a friend. My vibration rose, and now I actually do feel like a pillar of light, 'a conduit for the light of the heavens to the Earth … the rainbow bridge', to quote author Rebecca Campbell. I know I am here for a higher purpose.

****

For the next five years, I travelled regularly to London for check-ups and scans. Looking back, I don't think I ever realised quite how scary those five years of my life really were. I just got on with it but not without the unceasing support and love of a wonderful friend, aka 'the *Chevre Sale*'. Her nickname means the 'dirty goat', but I have no idea why! She would cocoon me in her cosy London flat every few months when I had my check-ups. Waiting for my yearly CT scan results was a truly horrific experience, but she made the unbearable bearable. Unfazed by my foodie fads, she religiously fed me cherry tomatoes, almonds and avocado for breakfast. She will always hold the dearest of places in my heart as the embrace that held me through that uncertainty and madness … and boy, did we have some fun along the way! A terribly awkward Valentine's night in the city springs to mind, full of the sad and lonely outcasts of London, including us, of course! The next day after eating an entire cheesecake from the posh farmer's market, we embarked on a double sitting at the cinema with the mother of all hangovers. Watching *The Wolf of Wall Street* was a step too far, and my 'dirty goat' ended up pulling a whitey and talking to the pigeons on a bench outside the cinema! Tricky times but with the help of dear friends, anything is possible. Thank you.

'I don't care if you lick windows, run into walls, or occasionally pee on yourself. You hang in there, sunshine. You're friggin' special.'

→ @fuckology

Anyone who has been diagnosed with a serious illness will probably identify with what I am going to say next. As soon as you shut your eyes at night and as soon as you open them in the morning, the demons appear. You can make yourself busy the rest of the day, but those two moments are when reality hits you and there's no escaping the pure paralysing fear that you might not make it. I found a mantra that got me through those moments. I would repeat it in my head, time and time again, like counting sheep until I fell asleep and then enough times to jump out of bed and get busy.

'Every day in every way, I am getting better and better.'

If I think about it, 365 days for five years makes an incredible 1,825 days of demon bashing with that mantra. Then 'puff', all of a sudden, it's over. On the five-year anniversary of my surgery, I went for my last CT scan – on Valentine's Day, of course – and was given the final all-clear. It was the most surreal moment and incredibly emotional saying goodbye to my specialist. It's weird to say, but the doctors and nurses at the hospital had become like family. I knew every doorway, corridor and lift like the back of my hand. It was a hideous but somewhat reassuring routine that I had followed for five long years, and suddenly I was being sent out solo into the big wild world. No more visits to the hospital. No more awkward 'wrong undies' moments. No more puke-inducing moments of waiting for scan results. No more tea and biscuits in the waiting room. I was set free.

My cancer is literally physically and mentally behind me now. I hardly ever think about the scar on my back unless someone comments on it, and the demons have jumped ship. I do see a dermatologist on a yearly basis who checks my moles and my children's, but that's it. I refuse to be pumped with radioactive material for a yearly PET scan which was once recommended to me. I am fit and well and will remain that way. And yes, for sure, every now and again I will get a reminder that I was diagnosed with cancer. Maybe a movie or a piece of music or a photograph. They are fleeting memories but hang around just enough to remind me how incredibly grateful I am to be here.

The Big C certainly changed my perspective on absolutely everything in life. It gives you this almost childlike awe and appreciation of every breathing moment. I can't really explain this to people face to face because it makes me feel cheesy the way 'hashtag #grateful' can sometimes make me want to smack someone! Does that make any sense? But it really did have that effect on me. Friends sometimes say to me, 'You have such a great life,' and yes, I bloody well do. Why wouldn't I? Why would anyone not live their best life? You only get one shot at it, so why wouldn't you put every ounce of energy into living your dream existence, taking risks and having the most amazing adventure? I'm living my incredible life to its fullest and won't settle for anything less than extraordinary.

So battle numero uno was over with and won! I can hear Terry Wogan now at the Eurovision Disease Contest ... 'Cancer, nil points!'

Now for a rather large rewind, as blow me down with a feather, but cancer was not the only battle that I had to fight at that time in my life. Battle number two was fought simultaneously, and here's how it all began ... from the Big C to the Big D!

'Sometimes you don't realise how fucked up someone treated you until you're explaining it to someone else.'

– @fuckology

THE OLDEST TRICK IN THE BOOK

'Oh fuck! What was that?' An almighty bang broke the peaceful sound of yoga music and trilling cicadas. Our dear old 1971 Mercedes Pagoda, fondly known as 'Pammy' (because she liked to get her top off!), had been driven into the back of my yoga teacher's car. I was in the middle of a yoga class in my hallway with some friends. My perfectly stable warrior pose was abruptly interrupted, and little did I know that I would need to become the 'humble warrior' for the foreseeable future. The oversized oak front door swung open and in he staggered, drunk as a skunk but still exuding his aristocratic good looks. The thick mop of blonde hair, those high cheekbones and that classic Belstaff jacket. I walked towards him and, with an all too familiar sadness in my eyes, took hold of his clammy hand and led him upstairs to bed. I tucked him in lovingly like any mother would do. The problem, or rather irony, being that this was my husband and not my son.

The girls promptly rolled up their mats and made tea as only two English roses would. At that moment, I had no idea that in less than an hour, my whole life would come crumbling down around my bare, bronzed feet. As the girls hugged me and offered loving condolences, I remembered I must find the keys. My ex-husband had a penchant for waking up in the middle of the night and heading back out on the town. As I'd done endless times before, I found the keys to hide them away, only this time his phone was in the same coat pocket.

It was the oldest trick in the book. Whoever she was had been saved under an old friend's name. Only it was highly unlikely that this mate would have declared his undying love for my ex-husband in a text message. I wondered for a second if my ex-husband had ever asked his friend for permission in this dastardly tale of deceit and adultery. The first and finest example of his inability to do bad things nicely. It was never so much a case of what he did but rather a case of how he did it. And I knew why. It was not his fault. The cord had never been fully cut. He'd never been allowed to become a man in his own right. He should have been pushed out of the luxury nest years ago as he would have soared, but this never happened, hence his inability to act alone without counsel from parents, lawyers and accountants.

I am
free

#ubudyogacentre

'No man is free who is not
master of himself.'
– Epictetus

The coming weeks were a complete blur, but I have one vivid memory. 'You know, Mummy, that Daddy is going to leave,' were the words my tiny intuitive daughter said in a very matter-of-fact way but in pure innocence. I remember exactly where she stood, at the corner of the rather imposing kitchen island, right by the wine fridge. Small and innocent but oh so wise. I brushed off the comment, not wanting to seem alarmed, but deep down, I knew that my acutely alert daughter was completely right. Daddy was going to leave me emotionally, and his children, their home and France physically. Sooner than I thought.

THE BOOK OF DOOM

The next part of my tale is the hardest to tell. I tried desperately to find an old diary of mine where I would find my raw feelings. I nicknamed it the 'Book of Doom' as it was ironically given to me by my ex, the Christmas he left me. A large leather-bound journal embossed with my initials in gold and a matching wallet to boot. I mean, you really do have to wonder why he felt this was an appropriate gift. I guess they were intended to cushion the blow?

The Book of Doom contained all the notes from our divorce along with many outpourings of anger, disbelief, shock, horror, betrayal and heartache. I used to hide it in various places around my house so that it was never found either by my ex or the kids. I have been unable to find it, and, well, maybe that's a good thing? I don't feel like I need to revisit those dark days of crying every single night for a year. Those feelings are no longer within me. They've been thrown down a flowing river in a large rock with an almighty cry. A process I thoroughly recommend, by the way.

Three days before Christmas, just a month or so after discovering the affair, my ex-husband took me for a drink in the cute village bar and told me he was going to leave me. Our family Christmas dissolved into a comedy of errors, a masquerade ball of deceit. Although I was trying everything I could to put on a brave face, the minute my twin sister clapped eyes on me, she knew something was up. The cat was out of the bag, and so I told her in just a few words what was happening, but there was no way that anyone else could know right now.

I sat by my ex-husband's side in his parent's home, where we had been invited, with our beautiful children running around oblivious to the fact that Daddy was about to leave and Mummy was utterly heartbroken and had been abandoned at the most crucial time in her life. I was in shock and incredulous that he could just carry on with both our families in one room, pretending that everything was OK.

On Boxing Day morning, I was in the kitchen with my ex-mother-in-law. My ex-husband had gone out for a run to escape the 'hideousness'. I can't blame him, really. She commented on the fact that he had given me way more Christmas presents than I had given him. I started to explain that actually he'd had his gifts at home in France, but my emotions erupted, and I burst into tears over the sink. I couldn't hold the secret in any longer, and I blurted out that he'd left me. Her reaction was the icing on the cake. I was longing for a hug, but instead, I was bombarded with accusations and questions about how she would see her grandchildren. It was the last straw for me, so I ran upstairs and called my sister to come and get me out of this ghastly nightmare. Still to this day, the memory of that morning is one of my worst. I have a son and a daughter who I love with all my heart, but if ever I am a mother-in-law (and I hope I will be one day) I have promised myself that I will never ever treat my daughter/son-in-law with such disdain. A mother's love is unique for sure, but to smother your children and defend them no matter what is simply unhealthy and delusional.

Not in a million years would I now submit myself to such humiliation and mistreatment. But I look back and smile a kind smile at my weak, scared self, whose world was crumbling at a rate of knots around her. She had gumption and pride even then, but she was broken and needed help.

What my ex-husband did to me was 'violent'. I realise that's a harsh word, but to be left by the man who had promised to be by your side (through sickness and through health) at the precise moment when you think you might die is simply hideous. The affair was just a by-product which didn't help the situation, but it was never that which mortified me. The sense of abandonment was crucifying. My sense of self-worth simply disappeared overnight. I was petrified, and on the odd occasion, my hands will still shake if I take myself back to how I felt. If not for me, then maybe for our two kids, you might have thought that he'd have tried to stick around a little longer?

'A wife is for life, not just for Christmas!' – a rather ironic line that I wrote to my parents in a distraught email during the year of our divorce.

FINDING MY FAIRY GODMOTHER

I am no longer amazed by life's coincidences. Instead, I marvel at life's perfect synchronicities, and it is one of these which I can say, hand on heart, helped to save my life. The morning after my ex told me that he was going to leave me, I pottered off to my regular Barre Pilates class, not knowing what else to do. I was in shock, but no one would have guessed from my cheery external appearance. I had always warmed to this wonderfully vivacious, stylish and funny woman in class. She had legs to die for, bright red painted toenails like me and a zest for life that oozed from every pore. Fortunately, my fondness for eavesdropping paid off as towards the end of the class, I overheard her telling another student about her website, and it became apparent that she was a counsellor. I grabbed her in the street after class, collapsed into tears and told her what had just happened. This remarkable human being took me straight back to her house, where we had our first session.

I hesitate to call it a session as that word does nothing to imply the absolute necessity of my time with this woman, who I fondly refer to as my Fairy Godmother. She was the fuel that I needed to fill up on weekly through the whole hideous sickly potpourri of cancer and divorce. I would arrive completely empty, with no perspective, at my wit's end, and leave with a full tank of energy, a plan of action, and most importantly, a smile on my face. I owe everything to her. There are simply not enough positive superlatives in the English language to describe the help she gave me and my children, who both fell in love with her too. When my daughter laid her head on our Fairy Godmother, you could see her physically relax, the biggest of exhales was audible, and we all knew everything was going to be OK. There is truly no greater gift than having this divinely talented soul in my life. She became a dear friend who I recommended to countless others and is still there for me and the kids today. Thank you, thank you, thank you, forever. You are one of life's angels. You taught me how to fight alone, to be titanium.

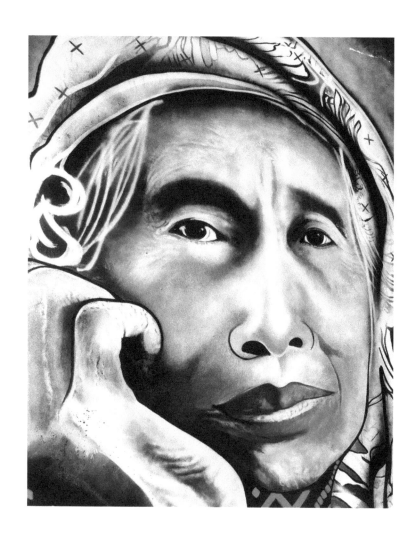

'When you've really suffered,
it brings you a gentleness, it has to.'

– Daniele Laporte.

This is one of the most precious emails I have ever received. It is a thank you note from a dear friend who I passed on my Fairy Godmother's details to. It touches me to my very core to hear the profound and positive effects that her help had on my friend.

'Dearest friend, partner, sister and inspiring soul,

There are no words to catch the feeling of thanks I want to send you.

In the space of 5 weeks, I have moved through layer after layer of illusion, confusion and disillusion to take me from the rocks of hopelessness to a place of strength, clarity and happiness.

Right now, as I write this to you, I feel solid, safe, powerful, brimming with potential, sure of myself, grounded in reality and content in a way that I remember from years back but haven't felt in over a decade.

I could never have done this transition so quickly or determinedly as I have without ****.

With ****'s guidance, I am better able to take the next best step each day. I am clearer and stronger for the kids. I can handle ****** (her ex) with love and compassion as one human being to another, without the tangles of hurt and fear guiding my decisions.

There is no greater gift we all could have received than the gift of ****, and to the end of time, I bask in love and gratitude to you. We all do.

What an impact you have made on our lives. What a partner you are to me. You are the definition of love, and I'm so lucky to have you by my side.

Thank you so much, you have changed my whole world and I've never felt better. You always have been and always will be a role model and inspiration to me.

Big exploding hearts full of love to you,

I could not put it any better myself, and it reminds me how important it is to share the good people who we meet in life. Word of mouth, recommendations, and praise make the world go round. Be generous with your treasure and the Universe will pay you back tenfold. I am sure of it.

'Sorry, I'm not Adele. I don't wish the best for you, nor do I want to find someone like you. I do, however, want to set fire to all your stuff.'

– @fuckology

TRUST YOUR INTUITION

Now back to my story and a third writing prompt from *Write On*.

Tell about a time you trusted your intuition.

This is the last piece in the 'puzzle of crap', and it's essential to finish off that episode of my life.

It was now a month or so after Christmas. Were my ex-husband and I sleeping in the same room still? Surely not, but I was lying in bed and watching him put on a suit. He rarely wore a suit, and when I asked him why he was putting it on, he said something about a meeting for a second house that we'd recently renovated. That's when I trusted my intuition, and I knew there was no such meeting.

Deep in my gut, something told me that he was heading off, there and then, to file for divorce. Oh my God! He was going to file for divorce in France without telling me because he knew that I would be entitled to less. Please excuse my language but, the fucker! I'd done some research and I knew all too well that whoever filed first would have the power to divorce in the country of their choice. The decision literally lay in the hands of the legal clerk and whoever handed that infamous piece of paper over to the judge first. My ex walked out the front door. I ran down the stairs like a lunatic and locked it shut. My heart was in my throat. I was utterly incredulous and my level of devastation had reached an all-time high. Not only had this man left me in the most spineless way three days before Christmas, but now he was filing for divorce without even telling me. We got married in England and that was where we should be divorced but as I mentioned earlier, he was under the trance of his 'superiors'.

I quickly phoned a solicitor in the UK. Funnily enough, they were the Queen's lawyers who represented our now King with his divorce. They were utterly professional and incredibly composed. They explained what documents I needed to gather and that they would move heaven and earth to try and get the court order filed first. Of course, the scanner and printer wouldn't work. I was at my wit's end. I phoned a dear friend who worked in an office. I knew he'd have everything I needed, so I asked him for help. I grabbed the paperwork, and off I dashed. But it wasn't meant to be. Despite everything we did and the help of those kind people, I didn't make it and my ex filed first.

I have this view in life that shit happens – it's not great, and sadly it's part of life as a human being. However, it's how you deal with the shit that stands you apart from others. At that point in time, I felt that my ex-husband's biggest talent was being able to do all the awful things in truly the most uncaring and painful way. I used to say that not only had he stabbed the knife in, but he also liked to wiggle it around as well. But at least I had tried. I trusted my gut and I was right. My friends helped me, and you know what, maybe it worked out for the best? Actually, retract that statement. It most definitely worked out for the best.

I found the most incredible lawyer in Paris who looked after me. She was the quintessentially chic French superwoman with her own law firm, mother to four children and wife to an English gentleman. She was elegant, in control, highly professional, but, at the same time, incredibly down to earth and empathetic with me. We worked together, and it soon became clear that I was actually quite good at negotiating directly with my ex, so often she would leave dealings in my hands. She encouraged me to fight to a point that was fair and then we left it at that. We could have continued, but she realised that battling for a year was enough for me. The regular trips up to Paris (often on the same plane as my ex-husband but sitting in different rows, of course!) were taking their toll. The babies were only four and six, so I used to put them to bed and then turn to my divorce paperwork and work through the night. It was relentless, but within twelve months, the divorce was signed and I could move on with the next chapter of my life as an independent single woman and mum.

My wonderful lawyer offered me a job in Paris! I was so flattered, but city life is not for me, especially with two little ones in tow. It's strange to look back, but as with the doctors and the hospital in London, I have a certain fondness when I think about my Parisian ally and my trips to the capital. I became very close to these people who I trusted implicitly and who, in turn, treated me with great kindness and humanity.

I was proud of myself for handling that episode with grace and dignity and can hold my head up high. There's not a single thing I would have done differently. I would like to add that 'the fucker' no longer deserves that name! In fact, he is now a good ex-husband and a supportive daddy who I will always care for as the father of our kids.

'Unfuckwithable:

adj. When you're truly at peace and in touch with yourself, and nothing anyone says or does bothers you, and no negativity or drama can touch you.'

– @fuckology

YOUR LOCAL TEA GENIE

So there I was. Divorced at 41. A single mum. Still battling with cancer but fit and free to start my life in a way I would never have imagined. I fought to stay in my home in France and that is where I lived for the next few years. Where on earth do you start rebuilding your life?

I started with paperwork. How glamorous! I had always left the bills, taxes, maintenance issues, and investments to my ex-husband, and now it was up to me. I dived right in, finding the best deals, changing suppliers, gathering a team of reliable work people around me. It felt empowering and so good to be fully in charge of my home and my budget. I found a financial adviser and put my trust in him completely, as financial markets are not my bag. Take me to the St Tropez market, however, and I can make endless great investments in bags!

I wanted and needed to earn my own money to be able to stay in my home in France, so I opened up my front hall for exercise classes, hosted restorative retreats and decided to rent my house out for the whole of July and August every year, something I still do to this day. I also started to import English tea for my ex-pat friends. I am a self-confessed tea snob and my favourite brand is Teapigs. Their little temples of the purest, freshest tea and flavourings bring me the utmost joy and one bag can last me all day with endless top-ups. The simplest of things, eh? Teapigs are also the most friendly and supportive company to work alongside and before I knew it, I had a garage full of tea which quickly became a firm favourite for my friends and my Côte d'Azur network.

It feels kind of strange to talk about my little tea business, but it was a pivotal time in my life. It became my cottage industry, so to speak, and a path to a wonderful community on the Côte d'Azur. It didn't earn me a fortune, but it provided me with purpose. It got me out and about and it gave me a much-needed identity at the time as the local Tea Genie, something that will always make me smile! I worked with a local nutritionist who promoted my tea with her cleanses. I packaged up boxes with traditional English biscuits or sweets and made gift packages which I sold at Christmas fairs and other local events.

I even supplied some of the superyachts. I remember my son helping me once, and I felt really proud that he was seeing his mum get creative and 'businessy'. It was a peaceful time in my life and very grounding.

The best of it was that it got me writing. I started writing regular emails to my customers, which quickly became an opportunity for me to write about life, my passions and my quirks. From adding Cinnamon & Apple tea to my Nana's crumble recipe, to linking Ed Sheeran's lyrics to Mao Feng Green Tea, to my favourite double entendre, 50 Shades of Earl Grey, my imagination was running wild. Who knew that something as simple as tea could be so therapeutic for me? I am still hooked on Teapigs to this very day, and I even travel with it. I guess you can take the girl out of England but never the English tradition of a good cuppa out of the girl!

I was the first of my ex-pat community to get divorced and it shattered my confidence. I remember getting ready to go to parties and feeling so incredibly nervous that I would try to think of the perfect excuse not to go. It's not like my ex-husband and I would be glued together when we went to social gatherings, but having him there in the background gave me a sense of security, I guess. Now I was on my own. I didn't feel I had much to talk about, which is ridiculous, but now I can sympathise with that woman. In fact, I would almost call myself a girl back then. I was figuring out a new way of life when everything around me seemed to be carrying on as normal. I was a mum but without a dad by her side. I was trying to make our home, my home. I was exploring what to do with myself professionally and personally and all the time with two little kids to bring up. It was a challenge, so no wonder I wasn't up for partying!!

I guess I just took one day at a time, and weeks rolled into months that rolled into years. I learnt a lot along the way. I learnt that I couldn't be Mum and Dad and compensate for when he wasn't around. I learnt that I couldn't control what was said or done when my kids were with their dad. I came to understand that I could only do what I could do, and that for me was to keep them grounded and loved and supported no matter what, no matter where. I came to appreciate that although they suffered immense pain, they also gained certain tools, such as resilience and adaptability, that would help them as they grew up. I witnessed the most beautiful unbreakable bond develop between my children that makes my heart leap from my chest. Those kids never ever fight. They simply adore each other and they have each other's backs big time. Blimey, I learnt a lot. I adapted. I got frustrated. I digested. I went easy on myself, and I moved forward.

'Those who fly solo
have the strongest wings.'

GOING SOLO

My ex-husband didn't fight for joint custody of our kids, which, of course, I was delighted about. At first, he lived down the road, and we all thrived on the routine of alternate weekends and sharing holidays. The kids still recall that time with so much fondness. Then he moved back to the UK, got married again, and there was no routine. He has always come to spend time with them but in different places, at different times. He had two families now, and I know he felt 'pulled from pillar to post', but it was his decision to move away. I think we've done pretty well most of the time at organising ourselves with our regular diary sessions. I am most definitely the 'default' parent, which I am very happy to be, but it sometimes feels like I am asking him to babysit. It's the oddest feeling because he's their father. Anyway, we see our situation in such completely different ways that we no longer speak about it.

Overall I am proud of developing a polite and caring relationship with my ex-husband. I decided from day one that the children would never be caught up in any shenanigans that went on between us, that I would never badmouth him in front of them and that as he is always going to be part of my life, I would do my utmost to develop a mutually respectful relationship.

The early years were really tough. I was still so bruised and yes, I admit it, I was jealous of his new wife and their extravagant holidays whilst I was at home with our two small children. Although deep down, I knew where I'd rather be. That glamorous life of ours and those superficial feelings of wealth and superiority had never fed my soul like my children do. It was tricky nonetheless, but as the years rolled on, we found a way to communicate that was honest. Now don't get me wrong, there are still times when I want to strangle the motherfucker! But I've found a satisfactory way to deal with my frustration or disappointment. Shall I let you in on my canny trick?

I write back to him with all my incredulity. Yep! I rant my head off, I swear, I let rip. There are many expletives involved. And then I leave the WhatsApp or email there in the ether. I know that the energy of the message will get to him. I don't need to press send. I leave it there to work its magic and then when it feels good, I press delete. I wonder if I'm avoiding conflict sometimes, but then I have known this man for twenty years, and I know that he'll never change – and what right is it of mine to try to change him? He is who he is. He'd be the same if we were still married (although I admit he would be more present). But his ex-wife having a go at him isn't going to change anything, is it? So why not take the more peaceful route and be poignant in silence? Arguments don't need to turn into disrespect or bitterness, but I have learnt with him that if I do answer his questions and give him my opinion, it generally does blow up in my face. He doesn't want to hear it.

Now my canny trick did go wrong once when I was sitting next to my ex-husband in the car. I have no recollection of where we were going and why we were together, but he had obviously really pissed me off. I messaged my friend with something along the lines of 'beam me up, scotty, jeez he's such a twat', pressed send, and immediately his phone went 'ping'!!! Oops! I'd sent him that message by accident. Well, he looked at me and actually agreed with me that time. So maybe I should press send more often?

We still have our spats, which is normal. I have incredibly high expectations of him, so really, he doesn't have a hope in hell's chance of my complete approval! I disagree with how my ex-husband does a lot of things, and I am one hundred percent sure that he feels the same about me. However, I know that if the shit hits the fan and I needed that man to be there for me, or he needed me to be there for him, we would be, and that's a pretty cool thing to say about a divorced couple. We have an unspoken impenetrable contract of respect that protects our children and our everlasting bond as their parents. It is so acutely personal and precious that neither of us can describe it to others and has developed as we have both grown and matured together (particularly my ex!).

If I had continued to carry around my negative feelings, it would only have been me who would have been affected. They would have slowly eaten away at my spirit from the inside out. I would most probably have got ill again, and it would have done absolutely nothing to change what had happened. There is nothing in my mind to be gained from holding onto negativity. It's absolutely pointless. Don't ignore it because that would be negating your always valid feelings, and you should respect them, but then be done, move on and put your energy into something way more important or exciting. Why give an ex-husband all your magical energy when you can give it to someone else?

BEAUTIFUL BOUNTIFUL BALI

A few years into singledom and life as I knew it would never be the same again. After a holiday to Bali, my daughter decided that we should move there permanently so that she and her brother could go to Green School, a magical progressive school built out of bamboo in the jungle. She pestered me for a year. I found every boring and practical excuse in the book to say no to her until one night, that incredible daughter of mine said something so profound to me that I knew I had to make this happen. She made such a powerful statement that her words are engraved in my heart forever. I don't feel I can share them here as they are intrinsically personal to her and could be easily misunderstood, but it reminded me that we get one shot at this wonderful life and it was time to take action. Isn't it just incredible how a few magical words can change everything? Within a matter of months, we were on our way.

For me, it was perfect timing, and I was ready for a fresh start. Not as a woman who had overcome cancer. Not as a woman who had got divorced. Just me. On leaving France, I had sign after sign that I was doing the right thing. I was following my daughter's, and now my, dream to live in a land where I truly believed much good would happen. Where our souls could sing freely. Where our bodies and minds would be nourished beyond our wildest dreams and things would change forever. It was my first step forward into the unknown, but I was beyond excited and confident, and the Universe gave me an incredible helping hand!

I was standing in the queue at the airport in France, about to board a plane that would take me to the UK, where I would meet my kids and board a plane to Bali. Out of nowhere, I heard the unforgettable voice of the builder/con artist who had caused me and my ex-husband so much pain. I'll never forget that jolting moment when my heart shot into my throat and my breathing quickened. I hadn't felt that feeling since we'd discovered what those awful people were doing to us all those years ago. What the hell was this man doing on 'my' plane? My immediate reaction was to ask, 'Why now'? Why was he here spoiling this special journey, the first step of my adventure? I scuttled

'I take a leap of faith not because I know I can fly

but because I choose to believe in what lies before me.'

@davidleppan

on board in front of him with my head lowered, sat down and pulled out my journal. Within a few minutes of writing, I knew exactly why he was there. It was the Universe showing me that if this awful man was back in France, I was doing exactly the right thing by leaving.

I soared into the sky, and a beautiful rainbow lay beneath me over the bay below. It was stunning and serene and by no means a fluke of nature. I was on my way. I was onto another chapter of my story to find another pot of gold. My heartbeat slowed and my face softened as I realised that I would have a safe journey to London to reunite with my children before starting our unforgettable adventure together.

We spent a mind-blowing few years in Bali, which changed our lives forever in the most profound of ways. I think the best way to give you insight into what it brought us is with some of the emails I wrote whilst I was there. I guess it was a kind of travel blog. I wrote this first episode after just a few weeks. I remember all those feelings so well. Every sense was being stimulated to an extent I had never felt before and which I now miss. I was starting to really live again. Not just survive but thrive!

'My mission in life is not purely to survive, but to thrive;
and to do so with some passion, some compassion,
humour; and some style.'

– Maya Angelou

EPISODE 1 – Selamat Siang ('Good Afternoon') from Bali

This rather momentous moon seems to be hitting me from all sides today. Firstly, with a restless night last night, then sending my kids off this morning in full ceremonial dress ready for a full moon ceremony at school – surely it doesn't get much better than that? Then from a full-on high-intensity hot Pilates class to an enlightening conversation with a new friend, to getting home and finally committing to writing some 'book', but then being totally compelled to do some form of mini ceremony and offering myself … not exactly a full Despacho Ceremony (an expression of gratitude) but a 'me version' that made me happy. Oh, my word and it's only midday! Then tonight, we are out to meet a Soul Sista and her beautiful family from France for dinner, which is totally surreal. Talk about honouring the goddesses of growth and unions! Boom!

So, Bali has scooped us up and is nourishing us beyond our wildest dreams. I spent the first two weeks on a total high … smiling my way through dreamy, balmy days. Hanging out at school and drinking coconut lattes, being welcomed by complete strangers, taken into the bosom of a family who we know from France coincidentally and relishing in the pure love between our daughters.

Then thwack! Reality set in, and I had a couple of 'What am I really doing here?', 'Will it ever stop raining?', 'Oh dear, are the children really happy?' moments. The constant stream of ants everywhere was no longer a novelty. The big juicy snail who likes to reside on my electric toothbrush wasn't amusing anymore. The mosquitos and relentless applying of spray and lotion became a chore. My son was on crutches yet again. Plus, looking like a greasy, white, bloated English tourist, sweating profusely with an afro that Jimi Hendrix would be proud of just about topped it all off!

We were warned by a wonderful counsellor at school that 'transitioning' isn't always a walk in the park, and I think I got my little dose just when I was feeling rather smug about it all. Now I don't want to sound ungrateful. This country is amazing, with the gentlest, most caring, genuine people I have ever met, but it's also a complete assault on the senses. Every sense is being stimulated to within an inch of its life from new smells, to getting used to the nightly chants of our resident gecko, to a new language, to the heat, to new food, to banking, to visas, to laundries, to my new best friend colloidal silver, to meeting an incredible number of new friends. It's all wonderful, but it's a lot and I was feeling F****** knackered, or slightly pooped, to put it politely.

So, I took myself off to the ocean (my big love) to let the kids run wild and just chill on my sun lounger. Well, they say a change is as good as the rest, and it worked a treat. My neighbours joined me, so the kiddies looked after themselves, and we got to know each other better across platters of falafel, holy moly guacamole and smoothie bowl heaven.

Now I think I've reached my happy place. I've got my local bearings. I've learnt to ride a moped so am mobile (although Mr Snail could probably beat me to the local café, in all honesty). I have the most wonderful yoga centre within a short walk which I am fully embracing. And best of all, some beautiful friends who are beyond helpful and kind and who already mean the world to me.

It's wonderful not having any crap TV to distract us. There's no washing machine, so you have to drop your clothes off at the laundry, no Netflix to stop me reading (I've read about 40 pages of The Mists of Avalon, which is a complete miracle for me). Plus, I haven't driven a car since I arrived, which is nearly a month … bliss. The kids hop on the school bus at 7.30 and are dropped off under the Banyan tree at the bottom of the road … so much better for the environment, and the hysterically raucous trip with Komang, the driver, blaring out his Top 10 tunes can only put the weariest of child (and adult for that matter) in a happy mood.

I realise that the one large living space that I've always craved is exactly how I like to live. Sleeping in the same room with the kids is the perfect excuse to retire at 8 pm (not that I need one), and waking up to their angelic sleepy faces and little warm bodies is a treat I must relish as they're growing up faster than I down my fresh coconut after my new found love, the Bikram yoga class.

I feel eternally grateful to their wonderful dad for giving us his blessing for this incredible adventure. It may only be for six months, but what we have already done and learnt in one month will change us and stay with us forever. I've been to Ecstatic Dance, discovered my inner creatrix, am a giver of long intensive, almost uncomfortable 'Yoga Barn hugs', thrown clay on a potter's wheel, walked in the rice paddies, fallen fully in love with my rice cooker, discovered the joy of properly sweating (and I mean wet through, sodden, stinky, dripping from every pore) then drinking a fresh coconut, being told such beautiful, special things about my children that make me proud beyond proud, learning, learning, learning each and every day and that's just for starters. Who knows what we'll have learnt by the end of June? If I ever stop wanting to learn, do give me a firm slap in the face, my lovelies.

On this very special Super Blue Blood Moon day, I want to send you lots and lots of love from Bali. May we all honour this special day in our own way, give thanks to the Goddesses of growth and union and become a little bit more aware of who we really are. Oooh I'm sounding all Bali already! Let's top that off with an OM.

Big sweaty kiss xxxxx

'Never stop learning
because life never stops teaching.'

Much like this little book, I remember writing and rewriting Episode 2 of my Bali story many, many times. I had so much to say. I can see exactly where I got passionate about stuff because of the detail I went into. It was like throwing a well-seasoned dry log onto a fire, my creative juices were ignited. I thought about cutting a lot of these emails out, but it seems disrespectful to the welcome that Bali gave me. It is well known that Bali either embraces you or violently spits you out in the first few months. I feel so privileged to have been lovingly accepted by the Island of the Gods, who not only allowed me but fully encouraged me to make it home. It's been three years since we left, but that life is still so tangible and there's so much I crave. As for the thigh comment, my older perimenopausal self just laughs. What on earth was I worried about?

Episode 2 – Bali Bodies, Self-Love and Writing

Good morning beautiful people,

I've written and rewritten this episode a gazillion times as I just seem to have so much that I want to write about. It's a bit of a hodgepodge, if I'm honest. I've been spending this week 'on Bali time'. It's an unusual concept to me, having spent most of my life feeling like I need to be busy all the time, achieving something or planning for the future. How often do I just sit and think without hopping up to answer the phone or answer an email, put the washing out or prepare tea? The Balinese are seriously awesome at 'taking it slow'. They walk slowly, they queue slowly, the pace of life is relaxing, and they sit. They sit and be. So, after seven weeks, I feel like I'm in the groove and life has just started to slow down, which is absolutely wonderful. The kids don't get dreaded homework, so our evenings consist of messing around on the soccer field with whoever may be there, a swim, a playdate, a read, an old-fashioned DVD and early to bed for us all. It's doing us SO much good and long may it last, no matter where we end up.

That said, I have just walked out of a pretty dynamic hot Vinyasa yoga class, having sweated out enough water to bathe a small child. Life isn't all lazing about. Hot yoga is something I never thought I would enjoy but I'm well and truly hooked. Unfortunately, the Ayurvedic doctor tells me it's bad for me right now as my 'Pitta' is out of balance; however, it seems he says this to most newcomers, so I'm going to slap some avocado on my Pitta and carry on! For sure, my body is missing its running, dog walking and Barre Xtend classes, but whilst I'm here in Bali, I'm feeling that yoga is the way to go.

It's possible that I will never again have this opportunity to practise daily from the gorgeous pick n mix which is available just five minutes down the road … Bikram, Ashtanga, Hatha, Hot Power Vinyasa, Kundalini, Inferno HiiT Pilates. I've tried them all. I love them all and what's more, my daily yoga is starting to take effect and doing a little bit most days really does work. Yes, gorgeous yoga teacher in France, you were right all along. My hips are more open, I feel stronger and more flexible, and it's a pure joy to feel these tiny yet significant changes after only seven weeks. Sadly, however, it's not affecting my physical appearance, and my body confidence has definitely taken a hit since landing in Bali. I'm going to be brutally honest with you now, peeps.

Fact: Bali is full of beautiful bodies – bronzed, toned, strong, flexible, cellulite-free, bouncy, enviable bodies. They are everywhere and very much on display due to the minimal clothing worn in this humid climate. Now I do realise that I'm no spring chicken and I would never compare myself to a 20 or 30-year-old, but I'm going to own up. I do have deep-seated issues with one part of my body, and that's my thighs. OK, so two parts! Confession complete!

I'm rather fond of my top half, and even the kahuna of a scar on my back doesn't bother me. My belly is a soft reminder of my two beautiful bambinos. Sure, I will never sport a funky ankle bracelet due to my 'cankles', but my little piggies are quite cute. My hair's 'interesting' but liveable with. My weird yellowy, greeny, browny eyes get attention, which is nice, and I got my teeth sorted last year, so I'm loving my smile. But those thighs! No matter what exercise I do or detox I undertake, they seem to have a life of their own. From just underneath my bum to the top of my crepey knees is a land unknown and inexplicable to me. I dream of a thigh lift. No implants, no Botox, no facelifts, no tummy tucks, but lifted thighs would be AMAZEBALLS. But who's ever heard of a thigh lift? So, you know what, it's one of those things that I just have to learn to live with and try to be kind to myself about – after all, they do a great job of holding me up. They help me ground deeply into the earth when I'm practising yoga. They move when I want to run and provide a lovely soft, ample pillow for my children to sit on. So, in actual fact, I should love them, shouldn't I, and appreciate them in all their glory right now because I'll look back in twenty years' time and wish I had. So last night, when I was massaging coconut oil into them, I felt a glimmer of fondness which I am going to try my hardest to nurture. In fact, I should be thinking that they're so incredibly sexy, they can't stop touching each other! (Get it?) And when I go running, they applaud me! And you bet your ass there's thunder between those thighs! Tee hee! And that is the beauty of writing. When you take a moment to really think about something, nine times out of ten, you turn it around or find a solution or a positive.

Now here comes another tangent, but bear with me! A couple of years ago, a so-called friend told me that I needed to be careful because women lose their looks when they hit 45. It's something that's stayed with me, and approaching my 45th birthday was rather nervous of, but now I'm well into my 45th year, I feel the need to strongly disagree. I think a woman in her 40s, 50s and thereon is utterly beautiful inside and out. We are a balanced, blended mixture of wisdom and curiosity, dependency and wildness, youth and experience. What's not to love? I'm loving this age and despite the state of those pesky thighs, I'm loving myself right now. Aho!

Which brings me rather conveniently onto Self-Love. We are surrounded by reminders, articles, and workshops about self-love and certainly, Bali has more than its fair share. But if there's one thing I've learnt over the last five years or so is that you need to love yourself first before anyone else will love you, and you cannot rely on someone else's love to make you happy. It's not their responsibility, it's yours. Whether you book yourself on a retreat, make yourself a nice cup of tea or simply massage your thighs, I would really encourage everyone to practise a modicum of self-love each day. Right now, my daily self-love is yoga and writing, and I love beautiful Bali for the time it's giving me to do this. I've also been dabbling in a few other practices that have included a workshop to 'Find Your Inner Creatrix', a breath and reiki workshop, a visit to an Ayurvedic doctor, Ecstatic Dance with the girls, a pedicure, but above all, giving myself time to write and putting my phone away and all other temptations is starting to happen … time to write my book, to write these emails, to stay in touch with friends, to write about the themes and intentions I will use when I teach Qoya one day.

I want to end this email by saying a huge Terima Kasih, 'thank you' in Indonesian. I was overwhelmed by all the beautiful messages that I received after Episode 1. You have no idea how much your words of encouragement mean to me. I now know that writing will play a huge part in my future. It's the trigger to my inner creatrix being at her very best, and so I am pursuing this love 100%, full throttle, pedal to the metal in both a professional and pleasurable capacity. It's funny because I started my working life as a copywriter and proofreader. I have always loved emailing and messaging and I seem to be able to communicate so much better with the written word, so it fascinates me that it has taken a whopping 45 years to come to this conclusion. Better late than never, eh?!

The weave and weft of life is coming together and starting to take form. Do I wish that I'd figured this out twenty years ago, perhaps? But then I wouldn't be the woman I am now and I wouldn't write in the way I write, with a tinge of sarcasm, a sprinkling of humour but above all, an immense appreciation for being here on this incredible adventure. With love to you all, Namaste and, of course, the obligatory OM.

Big sweaty kisses xxxx

The final episode that I want to include is probably the most important because I talk about Green School, which is the reason we moved to Bali. The effect of this place on my son, in particular, has never ever gone away. Since leaving Bali three years ago, there is not a single day that has gone by without him asking me if he can go back. Not one day! My boy found his 'soul home' and I have the utmost pride in him that he has not let this passion go. He might be a young teenager, but you can't ignore such a perpetual passion. I can't ignore the daily plea to return. It was his sister who got us there, and who knows, maybe now it's his turn …

EPISODE 3 – This is us!

Good morning, lovely peeps,

I should probably warn you this email is a bit of an epic outpouring. As you'll see, it put fire in my belly and got my juices well and truly flowing! I also want to say that it's just my opinion and how I feel right now. I have no intention of poo-pooing other people's opinions or approaches. Well, now that's over ...

I wasn't going to write about Green School just yet, but I turned on my computer this morning and a dear friend of mine had posted a video on Facebook that instantly fuelled my fingers to write this episode, and there's no time like the present.

Why did we decide to come to Bali? About two and a half years ago, we came to Bali to do a family camp at Green School, which we all loved beyond our wildest dreams. Climbing coconut trees, making our own rafts to get down the river, creating and planting giant scary scarecrows in the local paddy fields, tasting homemade chocolate sauce that we'd made from a cacao pod, making homemade dyes out of spices and vegetables to paint on our homemade paper with. All of this and so much more mixed with Balinese culture and tradition, living in a hut in the jungle, creating a wonderful community between us, sharing stories, laughing together ... it was magical. From the day we left, my daughter had decided that Bali was where we should live and that she wanted to go to Green School. She pestered and pestered and pestered me, dismissing all my weak and illegitimate reasons why we couldn't possibly move. One night she said something that was so poignant it took my breath away, and the next day I put the wheels in motion to move here.

From the deepest, most sacred part of my heart, I want to thank her. I now know moving to Bali is the best thing we could ever have done and there are a million reasons why, but one of the biggest is the school the kids go to – Green School.

BUTTERFLY PEA
Clitoria ternatea
BUNGA TELANG
Treats eye infections, acne, digestive cramps and urinary infections.
Use : flowers for tincture, tea, food.

'Tell me and I forget, teach me and I remember, involve me and I learn.'

– Benjamin Franklin

Green School is located on the banks of the Ayung River, about 20 minutes from Ubud, where we live, in the middle of the jungle. It is made almost entirely from bamboo. Ibu Leslie Medema, the Head of Academics, sums it up perfectly: 'Imagine this, a school without walls, a campus which ignites the senses and the natural curiosity of children, a place where innovation, creativity and learning flourish, a community, which has come together from all corners of the globe to share new experiences, a place of joy. Seeing children learning by doing, hearing deep and meaningful student discussions, experiencing daily growth as a whole person and feeling the joy of being part of a vibrant community of learners is the Green School experience.'

Green School's teaching method is not a haphazard, thrown-together, wing-it kind of approach. They have studied the best curriculums from around the world and cherry-picked the best bits to create a unique potpourri approach that focuses on 'hands-on learning', sustainability and moulding our children into responsible adults that are taking full responsibility for their planet and hence their future but in a really serious way.

Green School was built in 2008 to be a green vortex, creating green leaders because that's what this world needs, and kids have already graduated and are making a real difference.

An alternative to some of the cookie-cutter and 'box-like' schools in this world, kids are encouraged to think for themselves and question – why, when, how, what, who? They aren't drip-fed information day after day for the purpose of next week's test. There are no tests. They are exposed to learning in a 'hands-on' way – listening, seeing, reading, and, best of all doing. A wonderful example of this was my daughter's thematic class last term on Construction and Deconstruction when the kids were encouraged to pull apart everyday broken electronics that were being recycled, such as an iPad, a toaster, a DVD and a TV. They discovered how they work and looked at all the bits inside, where they come from in the world and how much energy is used to create these items, many of which we take for granted. With all the parts, the kids then created wonderful natural sculptures, showing how one world links with the other. Their teacher hopes that it will also give the kids more of an appreciation for the things they have around them.

If you have a maths class, then you might end up learning how to negotiate or estimate at the same time, great skills to grow up with. My son's class has been learning about planting and how the crops are grown in Bali, visiting a paddy field and also making their own rice paddy at school. He came home with a huge blister from digging.

This holistic and integrated learning environment for the students also extends to us parents. I am actively encouraged to spend time at school, and there is a whole area where parents can work with comfy beanbags, let alone three cafes where we can buy wonderful food from raw smoothie bowls to sauerkraut to local rice dishes to velvety matcha lattes. Every week there is a plethora of talks, workshops and fitness classes to choose from. This sense of inclusiveness and community is physically palpable when you walk onto campus. You probably won't even make it as far as the café without bumping into someone you know, and if you are sat on your own, then for sure a smiley face will strike up a wonderful conversation with you or, like I was on day two, whisk you off down into the jungle to the site of a new development of sustainable homes. Needless to say, there is never a dull moment, and the dream is really to bring the life of the children and the parents more and more together, so parents bring their skills and knowledge to school as well, and we all work, learn and create together.

The key to this wonderful environment is of course the teachers, who are all unique and incredible in their own way. Each class (that averages fifteen kids) has a main teacher and two assistants, including an Indonesian who is responsible for teaching local traditions and the language. The welcome that the kids get each morning is heart-melting, let alone the smiles and hugs I receive if I pop my head through the non-existent door and windows! I am bombarded with wonderful emails and updates about the kids' activities and learning in class but also their general well-being. As many of you know, my son is accident-prone, to say the least, so is a frequent visitor to the medical centre where not only does he get his wounds treated, but is where he was encouraged to sleep off his jet lag for the first few days after our trip to the UK. He didn't want to stay at home but staying alert in the afternoon was just beyond him, so off he popped for his naps. How wonderful is that? When my daughter missed the Year 5 drama performance in February, she was mentioned at the end for all her help with making props, even though none of us were there. The only way I can describe it really is 'family'. The genuine love, care and attention are an extension of the home that makes my heart sing with pure and utter joy.

The question now is, where do you put your children after they've been in such an incredible learning environment with such dedicated, inspirational teachers and children from all around the world? It's a conundrum that many Green School parents have, and that is why they end up coming over for six months and staying for six years! It makes us laugh, but it's actually a very serious question.

Now here's where I get passionate! I want to believe my children had a great start in life with their French primary education. Our village school was a good one, and there was never a day that they didn't want to go in. They have always been happy kids, but did they thrive and flourish and explore and question? No. They learnt from a book or off a board, but it wasn't applied to real life. They weren't really involved; they observed and got used to the 'sad faces' by the side of their tests or knowing they were bottom in class sometimes. In my mind, no child should ever be put in a line-up of 'who's the cleverest'. Surely that can only crush a child's confidence and desire to learn? I guess it taught them resilience if nothing else.

Does getting your 'b's' and 'd's' the right way around even matter? Why are many of our children pushed through their childhood only learning to answer questions for tests, tests and more tests? What does this achieve? Have I ever used the crop rotation information

I learnt at school? Surprisingly the answer is no. But maybe if I'd been taught it in a different way, relating it to modern-day farming, the challenges faced today and whether we could use some of the tricks our ancestors used and got to actually visit a farm and put my hands in the earth then maybe it would have floated my boat. Don't laugh, but I might have become a beekeeper or a vintner or a scientist in natural fertilizer or a researcher into sustainable crops. Who knows?

I want my children to relish in their childhood and take their time to figure out what floats their boats, which is only really possible when you've had the opportunity to explore, to question, to meet different people with different ideas, to spend time with yourself figuring out what you love and what's not for you. Every single human being on this planet is completely and utterly different, so why are so many beautiful, individual children being pushed to fit into boxes that crush their uniqueness, in places where the focus is on what they can't do rather than what they can do and where they lose their confidence? An unhappy, stressed child is never going to be successful. And what is 'success' anyway? I want my children to grow up knowing that their own happiness and health are the most important things. If they can feed themselves, make someone smile and help to look after this planet, then that is the biggest success in my mind.

I have been gifted with two extraordinary human beings who popped out from me chocca full of individuality, love, care, humour and creativity, and I do not want to put them in an environment where this is knocked out of them. I want them to grow up thinking they can do anything and go anywhere. They may want to go to university to study a subject that they have a huge passion for, or they may want to start a business straight from school or, in the case of my daughter, right now! She already has a book full of ideas and drawings for a business. She has already thought about how to involve the local community and benefit a local charity. She has a logo and has bought two domain names. She doesn't necessarily need exams to make this happen. What she needs is the confidence to push it forward, the resourcefulness to find the contacts she needs, the desire to get the experience required and an open mind to understand her market and adapt. As Albert Einstein said, 'Not everything that counts can be counted and not everything that can be counted counts.' Are 9 GCSEs, 3 A-Levels and a degree the only way to 'graduate'? I am often asked how kids graduate from Green School if they don't do any exams, so here is the answer.

Green Stone is Green School's High School final experience. It gives students the opportunity to demonstrate mastery of core skills and offers an extended period of focus on individual interests in an academic framework. It is designed and implemented entirely by students, based on their passions and interests. Each Green Stone culminates in a 13-minute presentation, in the spirit of a TED talk. They are filmed, edited and published to the world. But most importantly, these presentations are a rite of passage for all Green School graduates, bridging the Green School experience and each student's next steps in life. It is an opportunity for GS graduates to show the world what they can do and showcase their mastery of Green School skills which are adaptation, collaboration, critical thinking, creative thinking, thinking in systems, communication, activation and problem-solving.

So, you see, the emphasis is on experience and skills rather than credentials and standardised tests. Green School believes it is shifting the culture of education, creating sustainable solutions, and building bridges around the world. Graduates have been supported to develop as a whole person and with a good understanding of themselves and their place in this big and beautiful world. With a set of skills that will serve them well, regardless of their endeavour of choice. Their graduating pathways will be as diverse as the students themselves.

Well, you can't 'count' critical thinking or communication, but I know what I'd rather my kids had. I want my children to be happy and have a positive impact on other people in this world and, hopefully, on the world itself so that it's still a beautiful place for their children and grandchildren. I want them to laugh as much as possible and see that they can always laugh as long as they live. Yes, I know that life throws you a curveball sometimes, but there is always a silver lining, always. I want them to learn how to honour their bodies with healthy food, movement and mindfulness. My son asked me for real Aloe Vera the other day, which I had in the fridge. He didn't want the stuff in the tube. I love that! I want them to have the confidence to fly the nest when they're ready at whatever age that is. I won't be chucking them out just because they reach eighteen.

I know I want an awful lot, but 'until you spread your wings, you have no idea how far you can fly.' Green School has opened my eyes to a different way which currently nourishes me and my family in a way I could only once have dreamt of, and Bali has a big part to play too. The Balinese culture encompasses gentleness, peace, generosity and fluidity. There are smiling faces wherever you go. You really would be hard-pushed to be in a grump over here. They pray to be happy and that the Universe will continue to flourish, not for a new car or a promotion. The ceremonies and rituals ensure that the community stays united and comes together very regularly, and we are already feeling very much part of our little community.

I feel so lucky that my daughter felt so drawn to Bali. She knew all along that it is the best place for us right now, and what we have gained from Bali in only 3 months of our lives will stay with us forever. Life was pretty good before, but 'boom shakalaka' is life totes amazing now! We are being nourished inside and out and it's making us strong. Strong-minded, strong-willed, strong in heart and strong-bodied.

As Keala Settle says, 'Watch out, cos here I come … this is me!'

And as I say, 'Watch out, cos here we come … this is us!'

The six-month stay that we initially planned turned into two and a half heavenly years. Sadly, Covid came along, and we needed to return to Europe. I would have loved to have stayed put, but the kids' father and I co-parent, and airlines were shutting down, so I couldn't risk them being unable to see him. There was no way he was coming to Bali, so we returned in a horrific 48-hour pack and departure that still makes me feel queasy. We have unfinished business out there, for sure. We have wonderful friends who we were unable to say a proper goodbye to. So, I know we will return.

Our home in the South of France was rented, so we ended up in Devon, UK, where at least my son was able to surf. We lasted a year. Property prices and rental rates were soaring at an unfathomable rate. The world and his mother were moving south as working from home became the norm, so finding a long-term rental was like looking for a needle in a haystack. My writing stopped for a while, a sure sign I was unsettled. I didn't know if I was going to adapt to life back in the UK after 12 years, but what I did know was that this was yet another part of our journey, another chapter in our lives. It served a purpose for us all to realise that we missed our life in France. Finally, our house became available again, and that's where we've been ever since.

MY SOUL'S PURPOSE

All the travel, adventure, meeting new people and living in different places certainly had an effect on us. I feel, as a family, that we are way more adaptable now, and we have been left with a hunger for more. Our lives are richer, but we all crave to become 'billionaires in adventure'.

I can proudly and happily say that I am now middle-aged and utterly thrilled to have my health and my family. As for a career? I am, most definitely, still trying to figure out what I was born to do. What is my soul's purpose?

I have never had a career as such, just a stream of satisfying jobs. I've been extremely lucky and always loved what I've done, from being a PA to property development to retreat hosting to interior design to buying to PR and, most importantly, being a mum. So maybe I don't need to be asking myself this question? But you know when you go to a party, and someone asks you, 'What do you do?' … I never know what to say! I guess I can now officially answer that I'm a writer!

One thing I know for sure is that I love beautiful things. I am a true Libran in that respect. So perhaps my soul's purpose is to integrate spirit into matter? Oh, I can just imagine the look on the face of a first Tinder date when they ask me what I do and I answer with that! I adore bringing beauty to that which I touch, whether it's creating a breakfast, an altar, an outfit, a dinner, a home, a shop, a property, a holiday, an event … When I hosted retreats in my home, I wanted the guests to feel held like in the arms of the most devoted caring parent with all the luxuries they needed at their fingertips. I feel like I have the ability to work with material objects and awaken spiritual light within them. I hope that doesn't sound too big-headed. So maybe this is my purpose, my healing gift?

Objects are part of my life, of most people's lives, and I try not to feel guilty or frivolous owning them. Instead, I choose carefully, ethically and sustainably, where possible (although I really need to get better at that). I really cherish them, and yes, for sure, I do treat myself to a modicum of frivolity from time to time. Well, why not?

And that's what I envisioned when I started to write my tale. I saw a small, pretty book by your bed, easy to read, with a few laughs, some inspiring photos, lots of happy memories and hopefully a handful of helpful tips. A tiny book of positive energy and definitely not another 'Book of Doom'! I have always said that if just one person reads my story and gleans a glimmer of hope when they are feeling low or defeated, then my job here is done. That is truly my passion and my purpose. To spread positivity and smiles wherever I go.

'Leave a little sparkle wherever you go.'

THE MEN BIT

(oh and the thought of all those 'men bits'!)

I found myself single and ready to mingle. Maybe I should have been slightly daunted at this prospect after ten years with the same man but not at all. For sure, I was a little nervous. I've had my fair share of bad experiences with guys, but I always believed that there are endless wonderful male species out there, and I was excited to start meeting them.

I didn't have a whole lot of 'man experience' when I was younger. In fact, I was rather a late bloomer and was 16 when I had my first boyfriend, a piano-playing genius who wrote me songs and introduced me to the velvety voice of Sting. The pre-wedding years were neither a shag-fest nor could I have been labelled the Virgin Mary. So, there was plenty of scope to wander pastures new post-marriage, and I can confirm that I have woven a wonderful tapestry of 'man encounters', or maybe I could better describe it as a homemade patchwork quilt of many different fabrics!

One minute the quilt had an African theme. The next, a European vibe. It was a traditional English quilt for a short while. It took on an Asian look at times. Sometimes brand new, sometimes rather antique, sometimes designer and flashy, other times boho-chic. I think you're getting the picture. One of my soul sisters once labelled it my 'sacred sensuality' (more on that later), and I will love her forever for that beautiful, spiritual twist on what some might see as a bit of a 'shagathon'. I do have an endless ability for the deepest of connections when I need them and when the stars align, but then I can let them go too, with dignity and grace. I simply love men and spending time with men from all walks of life.

A conversation with a wonderful friend I knew a few years ago really struck a chord with me. He was kindly mending and adorning an old Balinese boat paddle with a stunning drawing of a turtle for me, so the double entendre of him 'sanding a paddle' made us giggle and led to a conversation of our mutual interest in the opposite sex. He explained that his aim, pre-marriage, had never been to have lots of sex with lots of women, but rather he was curious as to what it would be like to live with them, to go to dinner with them, to travel with them, to hike up a mountain with them, and I couldn't agree more. I love men in many shapes, sizes, forms, and yes, for sure, I love sex (well, good sex), but it's all the other wonderful moments that are just as longed-for: eating breakfast together, walking down the beach hand in hand, sitting opposite each other at a dinner party, watching a movie cuddled up under a duvet, waking up for a spoon, sitting beside them in the car, pouring two gin and tonics and not just one … the list is endless.

'She was never crazy. She just didn't want her heart to settle in a cage.'

– r.m. drake

THE YIN AND YANG OF BEING A MOTHER & LOVER

As a mum of two young kids, the practicality of dating was not quite so straightforward. It took me a long time to figure out the importance of how to get out of mum mode and into a state of 'lushness'. I used to try ever so hard, but having small ones meant I would have to physically be on a different continent to them sometimes to be able to switch off – or should I say, to switch on!

I definitely got better with time and then a few years ago, a wonderful lady, or rather guru, who helped me fast for a week on coconut water (which, can I add, included DIY garlic-and-coffee enemas twice daily), looked me in the eye and knew exactly what I needed to hear. She told me I needed to find my 'juiciness' and that before I went on a date, I should morph into a juicy lady. This is advice that has stayed with me forever and is responsible for two pairs of rather sexy lace undies that I bought on an impulsive shopping trip. One pure white and the other black, the yin and the yang. A reflection of my angel and devil sides. I bought them prior to a headily romantic trip to Oman, living proof that her theory worked.

'Oh, be still, my beating vagina!'

– From the movie *Mamma Mia! Here We Go Again*

But before Oman, this seems like a rather good time to remember some of the delicious and not-so-delicious male species that I have encountered over the years. You could say I've tasted it all, from Michelin Star to greasy spoon!

The list is long and luscious, definitely not in order, and let's just say, somewhat incomplete …

- My first kiss in Dublin post-divorce with a dashingly handsome Irishman who swirled me around the dancefloor and into the bar, where he kissed me long and hard.

- The suave, well-spoken, British-educated Asian who works tirelessly between London, Dubai, the States and Pakistan. He seduced me in Oman. His voice is like treacle. His sex drive is insatiable, and he works wonders for my self-esteem.

- The wise and oh-so-sexy Bosnian chef and restaurant owner. We literally set the bedroom on fire! We were so wrapped up in one another that we didn't notice the romantic candle had set fire to the duvet… there was smoke, there was drama, and a destroyed duvet was dragged to the shower! I will never forget what he said to me on our first date, and when he put his arms around me, I have never felt so safe.

- The Ghanaian prince who talked me into buying the most incredible grey sheepskin coat that has been much admired but also had me waiting on him hand and foot while he soaked endlessly in my bath. He devoured my banana bread like a beast with his hands, but it wasn't his hands that made my eyes water.

- The beautiful, gentle soul of my beloved Maori. His huge, firm body was covered from head to toe in the most exquisite tattoos, a story of his ancestry from a bee-keeping family on the North Island. So right in so many ways … a gentle, generous giant and a friend for life, I hope.

- The disco-dancing Londoner who snogged me in a Soho alley then ran an 80s-themed keep-fit weekend at my house in France in full fancy dress.

- The ever so funny and lovable Sikh. We sat for hours in a rice paddy field watching the fireflies. I wonder if we'll ever do that road trip?

- The American wine rep who gallantly flew in from the States and escorted me to a charity ball. That certainly was a bold move, as were his 'moves' by the swimming pool.

- The buff and bronzed American in Bali. The sex was ridiculously hot, but the chat was chilly.

- The Cornish local, eyes wide open, 'White Lines' and The Rocky Horror Show from the back of my Land Rover.

- The psychopathic narcissist from Mallorca who totally pulled the wool over my eyes and was flaky beyond flaky, yet how clever! I do hope the other women discovered what you were up to and that karma has paid you a visit.

- Ongoing flirting with the manager of a rather famous bar in Monaco and a few minor dalliances with the South African manager of a rather infamous restaurant in London.

- The cultured and devoted French man whose confidence I took for arrogance but who devoured me in ways I now dream of. More on him later.

- The other French man, a mummy's boy with a cultural chauvinism that left me uncomfortable but who sang to me in the shower like no other. More on him later too!

- The 6'6" giant whose bedroom antics were at times life-threatening, but his poetry could have earnt him Poet Laureate.

- An inevitable, flirtatious, post-separation '6-month' drunken snog with my ex at The Monaco Yacht Show, eeew! (It was hard to write that one down!)

- The ever so slightly bland yet utterly lovely Cantabrigian with his perfect house in the ever so slightly bland yet lovely English countryside.

- The sarcastic, adorable and artistic Aussie who I tried so hard to find chemistry with, but it just wasn't meant to be. He was perfect in every other way. Sporty yet cultured. Creative yet practical. In touch with his feminine side yet manly. That chemistry malarky's a bitch sometimes!

- The kind, log-chopping hunter in his tweed cap and plus fours who made a great fondue.

- The eccentric Monsieur Peregrine de Falcon (a nickname I gave to a well-heeled English fella) and his plethora of gadgets with whom I spent a wonderfully satisfying few days on a remote Indonesian Island. Naked for 90 percent of the time, we ate the entire contents of the minibar, thinking it was our welcome snack, and I drank his contact lenses by mistake! I remember watching the movie *Genius* with him in bed, which is about why we write and why we stop. I must watch that movie again.

- The extremely wealthy yet dodgy English office outfitter with a holiday home on the top of a hill in Mandelieu. He had oodles of charm but snogged like a washing machine. One night I intentionally knocked over a full glass of red wine onto my wooden parquet floor to avoid his repetitive lunges.

- The ex-SAS nutter who was leading a double life all along. A damaged soul with a husky voice and a huge belly!

- The 'punani melting' charming Portuguese who could have modelled for Ralph Lauren. If only we were younger, we would have had the most beautiful children.

- The salt-of-the-earth, entrepreneurial Liverpudlian who seduced me with an injured shoulder then drove me to Luton airport. What a gentleman. I still smile when I think of him, but he was still in love with his ex-girlfriend.

- The husky-voiced kite-surfer who lived in the coolest beach hut. I met him way back in the early days, so no way was I ready for a relationship, but we lay on an idyllic beach on the Poquerolles Islands, and I still remember today how it felt to fall asleep on his shoulder. I felt safe and reassured that life was getting better.

- The ex-rugby-playing Aussie who made a bonzer cheese platter and arranged the best dates. I love chivalry.

- The long and lanky paddle-boarding Français with the stinkiest feet and the messiest car. He looked so good in linen and bought me a tambourine.

'She was a little all over the place, that was for sure. But the good news is that when she loved, she loved big. And if she loved you, you knew she loved you. You never had to wonder.'

– Cleo Wade

THE ONES THAT GOT AWAY

A few of my lovers deserve an extra special mention. They brought and taught me so much. They had a profound effect on me, even though I didn't realise it at the time. They each helped me peel away the tough layers of protection that I had built up around myself after my heartbreak. You could easily have labelled me Fort Knocks back then or a really old red onion with layer upon layer of thick, acidic skin full of hurt and distrust and fear. It was never my intention not to be a young, juicy spring onion, it's just something that happened. These amazing men took me to uncomfortable places, places of pure joy and places of sad realisation. They helped to highlight the values that I now live by. I adored them all in one way or another and will always be grateful that I got to spend time with them.

Let's start with the first Frenchman.

It was his skin that I'll never forget and how he got under mine. The way he breathed into me so that my lungs filled with his breath. More than his breath ... his essence. It was intoxicating. It was so primal. All consuming. Raw. But I wasn't ready for it back then. I loved it and I wanted to give as good as I got, but as hard as I tried, I couldn't. He'd stick his face deep into my armpit and enjoy my stickiness and sweat. He'd push his head between my legs with no restraint. No airs and graces. He ate me up like a ravenous beast. He was animalistic and beautiful and his toned body knew exactly what to do. How to pleasure us.

I think he'd find me so different now. I'm truly in my body. I know myself. I love myself. I've healed and I'm thriving and I'm juicy! It would certainly be interesting to experience 'us' again. There's no doubt that the chemistry would explode pretty quickly. It drove him mad that I couldn't verbalise my desires, and that's fair enough. I tried so hard but I felt so uncomfortable. I have to thank him for the all-consuming love he gave me. He did nothing by halves, including our first-ever date.

We had matched on a dating app that allows you to browse possible love interests all over the world. The fact that we lived in different countries did little to dampen our online chemistry and when it came to arranging our first date a quick first drink at the local just wasn't an option. Even if it had been, this just wasn't his style. He was deeply romantic and perhaps somewhat of a perfectionist. He suggested that I fly up to Paris as he was there for business and could extend his trip. We daringly booked one hotel room with a sofa bed option in case we didn't 'connect'. He gave me a time slot when I could go into the hotel room to unpack and dress for the evening as he didn't want to 'see' me before our first date actually began. I'll explain in a moment.

It was so surreal to walk into a room and see his clothes hanging up and his toiletries already in the bathroom. We had texted extensively but never video-called, and I'm not sure we'd even spoken on the phone. That sounds crazy to write that now, but at the time, I wasn't worried at all – in fact, I was in a state of pure scintillating turned-on excitement. I went through his clothes to get a sense of his style and I smelt them. They smelt good and his bathroom accoutrements showed me that he liked to take care of himself. I pulled on my skinny black jeans and hopped into a taxi as I had to be at a restaurant at a specific time … not to meet him, but to be led into a pitch-black dining room called Dans Le Noir where you literally cannot see a single thing. It was exhilarating, and yes, I was a little apprehensive, but I also felt brave.

I'd been sitting down for maybe five to ten minutes, sipping my red wine and desperately trying not to knock it over. Suddenly I felt a presence beside me. He said my name. I must have said something back as he immediately located me, I felt his warm hand on my leg, his full lips on my lips, and we were kissing for the first time in total privacy yet surrounded by loads of people! Now you don't go to Dans Le Noir for the culinary experience. With no sight at all, you really have very little idea what you are eating, but all your other senses are heightened to heavenly extremes. You feel every breath, the slightest touch gives you goosebumps, and every word is crystal clear. As we finished our dinner, it dawned on me that I was going to meet him again. A double date with the same guy, sort of! I was finally going to see the man who I had already heard, smelt and touched. I became nervous, which I hadn't felt in the dark. We emerged into the foyer of the restaurant and I'm sure I blushed as he looked deep into my eyes and suggested we continue with cocktails at a nearby roof terrace. His confidence was intoxicating, his sex appeal potent, and I was under his spell. He held my hand tightly and I let him lead me through our first night together. What an incredible experience that was, quite possibly my best-ever first date. (And no, the sofa bed was not required!)

He continued to make supremely romantic arrangements for us to meet. Surprises that rendered me speechless, like booking a one-way ticket just so he could sit with me in Departures at Amsterdam airport and wait with me for my plane to take off. He made beautiful sacrifices for me too. But we rarely laughed. In fact, we found it hard to chat. Easy banter just wasn't there between us. From day one, I knew it wouldn't be forever, but lust and love got the better of me. Do I regret it? Not one bit. I will always love those chunky feet, that pert bottom and his man bag. He now continues a bromance with my dad, which makes me extremely happy, and I find it rather lovely. Maybe I was a gateway to a long, cultured friendship of mutual adoration between these two men? They have conversations about art, history, music and culture that I could never indulge either in. But I don't miss the arguments. He used to bring out a side of me that I didn't know existed. A petty side. A nit-picking nastiness that just isn't me – or was it good for me to shout and express myself finally? Hindsight is a wonderful thing …

He wrote me this love letter. Such beautiful words that I will cherish forever, 'Un matin je m'étais réveillé, tu dormais encore couchée sur le côté, le drap reposant à fleur de peau ne te couvrait que partiellement et je devinais sous lui chaque partie ce corps que j'avais tant étreint la nuit dernière. De ci sortait ta jambe, de là ton torse, ton épaule, son omoplate et sa cicatrice que mes lèvres ne se lassaient d'embrasser. Le soleil brillait déjà fort et à travers les tentures était un halo de lumière sur le lit. Ta peau était belle, sucrée, chaude... Et je me suis dit ce matin là que je t'aime et plus jamais je ne voulais me réveiller sans t'avoir à mes côtés.'

I'm not sure my translation will do it justice, but I'll give it a shot. 'One morning, I woke up, you were asleep still on your side, the sheet on your skin covered you only partially and under it I imagined every part of your body that I held so tight last night. A leg, your torso, your shoulder and its shoulder blade with its scar that my lips never tired of kissing. The sun was already shining brightly and through the curtains was a halo of light on the bed. Your skin was beautiful, sweet, warm, and I said to myself that morning that I love you and never again did I want to wake up without having you by my side.'

A second French man used to make me roar with laughter. My big bear of a man who loved me for kissing his giant feet in the morning. His one-man singing extravaganzas in the shower were a pure joy. He made love with an animalistic rawness. He was a big man. He'd sweat and he'd huff and he'd puff and I loved it. Making love isn't about what it looks like. It's not how it looks on television or in movies. If he needed us in a certain position, he'd get us there with his strength, not caring how it looked. He well and truly left his mark with amazing sweat rings that have never left my headboard! But the snoring was thunderous and relentless. In the early days, I told myself it didn't matter. I fell quickly and heavily in love with him. But it drew a wedge between us. I used to escape to the spare room, which is no way to start a relationship. In fact, it's no way to go through a relationship at any point. Physical closeness, a night-time kiss and a morning cuddle are essential for me. He did develop the most beautiful bond with my boy, who he just adored. He showed up in the hospital when my son needed urgent hand surgery, then scooped us all up, took us home and fed us – sushi for us, and for my son, the best steak he could find to help him heal. He was always so thoughtful, extremely generous but also oddly and inexplicably unreliable. Sometimes, he just wouldn't turn up and I just couldn't cope with that. It made me feel worthless. I would have loved for that relationship to continue but I think I was too independent for him. But now I look back and I understand. He was teaching me that I could start to rely on someone again. He wanted to look after me, but I just didn't feel safe enough with him. I went against his wishes and visited Bali just after the volcano erupted. We never recovered and that was that. I left for Bali a few months later without him.

My marvellous Maori.

An excerpt from my diary explains how I met this wonderful being.

He's the one I vividly dreamt of that afternoon in Dubai airport during an unexpected delay. It was a sign. The man in my dream was a Maori with tattoos. I remember him so vividly. Then I turn on Tinder upon landing in Bali and there he is. Naturally, I swiped right, and to my joy, we matched. Unfortunately, he was on a big trip home to New Zealand and Tahiti. We stayed in touch sporadically, but there were times when I didn't hear from him, and I automatically found myself thinking, 'I wonder if he's gone off the idea?' or 'I wonder if he's met someone over there?' But I was listening to The Secret at the time, and it reminded me time and time again to think positively about him. I did one hell of a lot of manifestation. I really went to town and it's something I'd never done before. When I went to sound healing at the Pyramids of Chi (Ubud, Bali), he was the loud, powerful gong that I kept hearing in my left ear like a roaring lion, reminding me that he was on his way home for me.

Written three to four months later.

So what have I been up to? I've been falling in love again. I met a beautiful, gentle giant surfer dude from New Zealand and from the day I met him, we have rarely been apart. It's been a whirlwind but a whirlwind that feels totally comfortable. He is loyal and deeply caring. He has a wonderful culture being Maori that he is sharing with us and the seriously sexy tattoos to match!

He surfs with my son, and the joy that I get from seeing those two in the water together and hearing him shouting, 'paddle, paddle' with his lilting Kiwi accent makes me smile from ear to ear. My daughter has taken her time to suss him out as is her way in life, unlike her mum, who jumps in with two feet, all singing, all dancing! I have witnessed moments of great intimacy between them when she talks about school and where she feels she 'should' go.

At times I've felt judged for going too quickly with this relationship, but how do you take it slowly when you're middle-aged, living in Bali, and your wannabe boyfriend lives two hours down the road from you? I don't have a babysitter or family to look after the kids, so it was kind of all or nothing. Someone even asked me if I'd known him from before as we seem to be so settled. I guess there's no right or wrong. Every relationship is different, and I should stop judging myself. Of course, I have a fear that it won't last and then the guilt that the kids have met him and that will come to an end, but I can't live my life wondering, 'What if?'. When I asked my daughter about him, she said, 'I just don't want you to get let down again, Mummy,' which took my breath away. My beautiful girl with her enormous heart understands the pain I went through all that time ago, and although we have both forgiven, I guess we will never forget.

Our relationship ended partly when we visited Europe together. It's such a weird thing to experience, but it just didn't work for us when we changed our surroundings. I think I maybe felt responsible for him, which of course is normal as we were on 'my patch', so to speak. It's sad and I know I wasn't particularly patient with him, and for that, I am sorry. He was also thinking about moving back to New Zealand. He will always be a special friend to me and my kids. He reminded me how it felt to be a family. Somehow it does feel different with two adults. It felt exciting and safe at the same time. I miss that feeling.

'Vulnerability, having the courage to show up when you don't know the outcome.'

– Brené Brown

'Good judgement comes from experience. Experience comes from bad judgement.'

MY SACRED SENSUALITY

Blimey, that is quite a couple of chapters! Cupid has been and continues to be kind to me, and I should really give a big shout-out to Tinder too! Do I read that list and feel like a hussy? Hell no! I read it and smile my cheeky smile. How extremely lucky I am to have experienced so many wonderful, varied men. It brings a wealth of joy to my life and it keeps my juiciness alive. I am the most devoted of mums, but I am also a red-blooded woman with desires and I never want to lose that part of myself, which is all too easy to do when you're doing it mainly alone. Life is for living, and sex and love and kissing and desires and snogging and fondling and foreplay and orgasms are all a wonderful part of that for me.

One of the things I like about myself is my ability to be able to open my heart without fear. I'm not cautious in love. Yep, that could be the understatement of the century! I jump right in, two feet first, with great gusto and red pumping hearts fluttering all around me. As I mentioned briefly before, I once picked a card that described this as 'sacred sensuality'. I didn't understand it, but one of my dearest friends looked at me as if it was the most obvious thing in the world and told me that I was the only person she had ever known 'to have let men come and go over the years. Let them be who they are. Let them go when it is necessary. And to do it with dignity.' I actually wrote this down as it was such a revelation to me and was the polar opposite of how people would joke about 'all the men in my life', which really made me feel uneasy and frivolous.

These men have not only brought me an abundance of sexual joy but so much more ... from falling asleep on a sun-soaked hot shoulder on the beach, to riding a motorbike around the Italian countryside, to walking Le Cinque Terre in Italy, to sitting in a rice paddy and watching the fireflies for hours, to drinking gin on a daybed under a mosquito net, to receiving a ring (not an official engagement but near enough), to wondering if he's a drug dealer, to celebrating New Year together in Dubai, to making my kids laugh, to bringing me a cuppa in bed, to clandestine rendezvous in hotels across the world, to eating pizza on the beach in the Maldives ... There are endless magical moments that have brought me feelings of desire, safety, happiness, purpose, companionship, butterflies, anger, bemusement, completeness, sadness, loneliness … the list is never-ending.

I am good on my own. I can hold my hand up and give myself that accolade, but I adore being in company. That strong arm around my waist, those soft lips upon mine, the scent of masculinity, the seduction and the laughs, from the everyday to the extraordinary … thank you to each and every one of them.

'The cave we fear to enter
holds the treasure we seek.'

– Joseph Campbell

THE GLAMOUR VS THE UNGLAMOROUS TRUTH

I am a 'glass half full' kind of girl, for sure. In fact, I would say my 'glass runneth over'. When I read my story, it's full of adventure, laughter, love and glamour, but I'm acutely conscious that I don't want this to underestimate the devastation that divorce/separation/abandonment, whatever you want to call it, causes. I think it can be sugar-coated all too easily.

I remember thinking a couple of years post-divorce that I was fully 'recovered', so to speak, but that is just so untrue. If I'm being honest, it took me a good five years to really feel confident and content with who I was, to fully trust again and to let down my guard. The repercussions are huge and still impact every single day of my life, yes, EVERY SINGLE DAY OF MY LIFE. I have never felt like a victim, and I really hope that I have never acted like one, but this is a simple truth.

'You may not control all the events that happen to you, but you can decide not to be reduced by them.'

– Maya Angelou

Being forced to spend time without my children is awful. I understand that I get time for myself which many parents dream of, and I make the most of it for sure, but it's not fair that I spend half of all their holidays and every other Christmas without them. They grow up so quickly. That's not what I signed up for when I decided to have babies, and these repercussions will continue for as long as I am alive.

The energy involved in managing life as a divorcee is huge, and I send all my admiration and love to those parents in the same position as me. I now have a good relationship with my ex, but sometimes it is still hard to talk and to agree. So, I can only imagine how consuming it is for those parents who have a difficult or non-existent relationship with their ex-partners. Huge respect is due, it really is. Heartbreak is hideous, and combined with divorce and cancer, I was rocked to my core. I don't say this for sympathy, it's a fact.

People often ask me how I coped. The truth of the matter is that I didn't do it alone, and the only piece of advice that I am 100% confident in offering is to find a counsellor, therapist, shrink, psychiatrist, whatever you would like to call them, but a properly trained professional to help you. This is heavy shit and you can't go it alone. The help of a trained ear will enable you to change your perspective when it's required, to dig deep when your reserves are empty and find balance, which is crucial. You are never going to come out of this event as a gold medal winner but you need the capacity of detachment to see things as they really are and not how you, the 'casualty', want to see them.

This element, the 'capacity of detachment', was my superpower, and it helped me so, so much. I didn't create a false reality, but instead, I had the courage to look into the mirror and see what was really happening. I believe that only a professional can help you to do this. Friends are wonderful, but it's actually not fair to impose your woes on them. They are too emotionally involved so can't be objective, and anyway, they generally have their own shit going on, so don't weigh them down even further with yours!

Don't you love that moment in the movie Zoolander when Derek looks into the puddle and asks, 'Who am I?' I have asked myself this question countless times. I've looked in a mirror and spoken to myself too many times to mention.

Some things I'm sure of. I am a mother, a carer, a nourisher, a host, a safe hug, an adventurer, a lover, a writer, an optimist and, although it makes me feel uncomfortable writing it, in my own funny kind of way, a hero. Cue excruciatingly awkward cringe feeling! But a few people have told me this, which of course, my ego loves. I listen and acknowledge the compliment, but I'm an English lass, so shouldn't I be humble and play it down? 'Oh, don't be silly, I just did what any other woman would do, right?' Actually, wrong. And here's another reason why I wanted to write this story, to try to explain this.

I did do things differently. I did them with grace and determination. In private, or rather with as much privacy as I could find. I was titanium, and that awesome tune by David Guetta and Sia became my anthem. I was wounded, but then I became 'bulletproof', walking through the battlefield with one child in either hand. (If you don't know this song, stop what you're doing and look up 'Titanium'. You'll thank me.) I like to picture Wonder Woman in her full sexy, glorious body armour, that no one could penetrate until I allowed it. I got wounded a lot. I fell down a few times. I was too tough, which made me weak again but I kept on walking, and I made it to the other side of the battlefield to wonderful, spiritually nourished freedom. I paid my dues. I was released by the Universe and took off. I can honestly say that five years after my divorce and cancer diagnosis, my journey went into overdrive. I finally felt free, properly free. I spread my wings and there was no stopping me. So, yep, it took me a long time to come to peace with what happened, but bitterness only destroys you, no one else and as Marilyn Monroe once said,

'Sometimes good things fall apart so better things can fall together.'

My trip to Oman is a prime example of a truly 'good thing falling together', so now seems like the right time to include a story about my incredible adventure in Muscat.

After my cancer, I promised myself that I would jump at any and every opportunity that life offered me, and I stuck to my word. Oman was just one of many adventures, but my first solo transatlantic trip which was a huge deal for me and it certainly did not disappoint. It was a last-minute, indulgent decision which I must do more of.

OH MY OMAN!
A TALE OF THREE KINGS

I can feel my heart beating as I write this chapter about my adventure to Oman. It just goes to show what an immense and lasting effect this trip has had on me. Did I fall for this beautiful, mystical country? Yes. And was I left wanting more? Quite definitely. Isn't that the perfect way to leave a place … satisfied but left wanting more? Like a good lover?

Let me start at the beginning. I found myself with five days and no kids. I could have quite happily stayed at home but a desire was bubbling inside me, a desire to go somewhere completely different, a desire for mystery, for culture, for the unknown. Then it came to me. I should visit Oman, the home of my only addiction – frankincense. This was the perfect opportunity to have a 'grown up' holiday, wandering through the mosques and souks in tranquillity,

taking time to sip tea and wine and indulge in dates and halva, a time to sleep on my own, to read, to write, to meet strangers. So, Muscat-bound I was and it totally knocked me sideways. The beauty of the tiny morsel I experienced, the warmth of the people I met, the vibrant colours, the intoxicating smells, the scenery, the food and the company. I had the most indulgent time and met three unique and enchanting gentlemen on the way.

Arriving at the rather divine Kempinski Hotel in Muscat at the rather undivine hour of 4 am, having travelled more than 15 hours, I was somewhat bleary-eyed, but the serenity of the striking entrance lobby with its lofty white pillars immediately enveloped and soothed me. I drifted up to my room, where I ran a hot bath, then disappeared into a cloud of white fluffy pillows for a few hours of wonderful deep sleep, exactly what I needed.

During my first day in Oman, I couldn't help but notice the 'chic sheikhs' or gentlemen floating effortlessly in long white ankle-reaching robes called 'dishdashas', always looking cool and distinguished with their immaculately groomed beards and topped with an intricately embroidered hat, a 'kumma', or a cashmere kerchief or turban known as the 'massar'. Seeing the women walk around in their long black 'abaya' dresses and 'hijab', the typical Muslim head covering, I got glimpses of fancy shoes and designer clothes underneath which made me realise there is so much more than meets the eye in countries such as Oman. I longed to know more about the culture that lay beyond the immaculate orchids and polished floors of my luxury hotel. There were riches that I knew I would find, and above all, I was on the hunt for my beloved, intoxicating frankincense in all its wondrous forms – the resin to burn and chew and the oil to dab indulgently on my skin. Oh, that heady, musty smell that transports me to a place of mystery, of calm but with immense clarity … a dangerous place, some may say, but religious leaders for millennia have affirmed that burning frankincense is good for the soul and I have to agree.

It didn't take long for the magic of Oman to start to seduce me. I was lying by the pool on my first day when an incredibly dashing Asian gentleman approached me and introduced himself. I was immediately captured by his velvety voice and immaculate Queen's English. I felt somewhat vulnerable in my black string bikini, but his charm worked quickly and before I knew it, we had agreed to meet for a drink at sunset. It was exciting to get dressed up, and I definitely had a little flutter of nerves as I went down to the dimly lit beach bar to meet this mysterious gent. I quickly learnt that he was based between the Middle East and London, working in finance. He was utterly charming and seductive, and one drink led to another as the warm breeze drifted over us and the gap between us on the couch became smaller. We shared some local crab and a rather lovely bottle of Chianti as the night passed in a flash. We agreed to have dinner the following night too, venturing out to a local restaurant, the Bait Al Luban or the rather aptly named 'House of Frankincense'. We dined on local seafood and drank frankincense-infused water before returning to our beachside spot for a nightcap. He was from such a completely different world to me and utterly fascinating. I couldn't have asked for more appropriate company. He was curious and interesting and sexy as hell! I feel sure that our paths will cross again, maybe in London, the Middle East or the Far East, where he often travels for his work.

The following morning, I was met by the immaculately presented Ahmed, my guide for the day, who drove me straight to the Sultan Qaboos Grand Mosque, which can only be visited between 9 and 11 in the morning. This stunning building can hold up to 30,000 worshippers, and I can only imagine how that might feel. Even though it was empty, the mosque brought tears to my eyes. I covered my head and chest with a shawl and followed Ahmed through the mesmerising arches and corridors, then into the main room with its 'make-believe' carved and gilded roof and second largest chandelier in the world. Simply incredible! I was lost for words. We then visited the Muttrah Souq, where I definitely experienced the dynamism of typical Omani day-to-day life. It is one of the oldest markets in Oman, dating back about two hundred years, and this history sucks you in as you start to wander its narrow paths. It was bustling but not crazy. Each shop owner tried to lure us in, but Ahmed guided me cleverly. He knew I was interested in shawls, something locally crafted and, of course, my precious frankincense. My eyes bulged as we walked past piles of beautifully coloured cashmere, stacks of the locally embroidered caps, window upon window of old silver and through clouds of frankincense. It was simply intoxicating and an assault on all my senses. I had asked Ahmed to help me haggle and he didn't let me down. He turned out to be a demon haggler, getting over 70% off the asking price, but he was fair and bought from people he trusted. I was pleased to have him by my side.

He helped me pick out the best dates, advised me on which old Omani silver earrings suited me best and found me the finest, whitest frankincense resin at the most incredible price. A gem amongst a souk of gems. I returned mid-afternoon laden down with treasures for myself and my Christmas list happily ticked off. I was ravenous and eager to write about my tour.

Emanuel, the delightful Italian concierge, recommended that I relax in the downstairs lounge. He ushered me down a glass spiral staircase to the wonderfully light and sophisticated tea lounge. A rich space full of walnut, velvet in muted neutral tones, with a highly polished cream marble floor perfect for the outside light to bounce off but not too bright and no glare, thanks to the cleverly tinted floor-to-ceiling windows allowing me a stunning view across the gardens and infinity pool to the sea. My afternoon tea exceeded all expectations. I indulged in the Wadi Cheesecake, a signature dish and homage to the Omani patrimony and landscape. The idea behind this cake was to have in one recipe some of the main ingredients you can find around the Wadis, such as dates, coconut, goat cheese and spices. The main elements in the Wadi are represented in the cake as such: the earth by the brown date biscuit, the water by the white goat cheese mousse, and the boulders by the pieces of crumble. A Wadi is a valley or ravine that can often be dry outside of rainy season, but this cheesecake was anything but dry. I think I might have experienced my most elegant afternoon tea to date (get it?!), especially when the grand piano started to be played. Elegant glamour, rich surroundings, 'financier' cakes, madeleines and choucettes under glass domes … mmm.

'Travel far enough to find yourself.'

The next day, early doors, I was picked up by Al Ruby, another rather dashing guide. My initial impressions were that he was a wannabe Indiana Jones, in his rather swanky 4x4 with Aztec seat covers. He wore the traditional Omani scarf wrapped around his neck in a rugged way and spoke quickly and confidently, introducing himself with his full name, Ashraf Mohamend Ibrahim Al Ruby. I had to ask him to repeat it several times, and I wondered which part I could use to address him. He smiled when I told him my name was simply Abi. I smiled at myself as we set off to the husky tones of Vasco Rossi! Not what I was expecting to hear on my adventure across the breathtaking Al Hajar mountains. I asked Al Ruby if he liked Italy in my basic Italian, and he immediately broke into beautiful fluent Italian, explaining to me that he was completely in love with 'all that is Italy' and had therefore taught himself the language. He specialised in guiding Italian tour groups on trips around Oman.

Al Ruby told me he was also an archaeologist, having discovered relics in the Coliseum in Rome and the pyramids of Egypt. So maybe I was right? I had a real-life Indy on my hands – how thrilling, and let's just say the flirting began almost immediately. I was more than happy to be the hero's female love interest in today's movie, and he could save me from the Temple of Doom anytime! On our two-hour journey from Muscat to the Wadi Shab, Al Ruby told me about the history of Oman, the religion, the Sultan Qaboos 'e tutto in Italiano', my favourite language in the world … well, I was putty in his rather rugged hands. As the day progressed, Al Ruby became more and more 'at ease' with me, a hand on my shoulder, an arm around my back, helping me climb up and down the rocks as we made our way along the ravine with its steep sides to beautiful clear pools. I welcomed the water as Al Ruby was pretty fit and was enjoying a speedy ascent while I was hustling to keep up! I immediately stripped off to my bikini, sadly without Al Ruby, and plunged into the cool water, swimming upstream, squeezing between incredibly tight gaps in rocks and ending up in a breathtaking cave with a waterfall inside. Wow, wow, wow … this was one of the most stunning experiences of my life.

Al Ruby scooped me up out of the water, asking me to dress quickly as we were off for a lunch of fresh kingfish covered with turmeric and red chilli with perfumed rice and a simple salad. I was starving and very happy to up the pace on our return to the car … 'No need for the gym today,' I thought to myself. Lunch was the simplest yet most delicious meal. I enjoyed serving Al Ruby his food, and we chatted about his love of cooking pasta, of course. I felt just like Julia Roberts in Eat Pray Love! Was this really happening to me? Was he for real? You know what? It didn't matter. I was having the time of my life, flirting, chatting, giggling and loving every minute. It was good to feel the woman in me. I told Al Ruby about my addiction to frankincense and that it was the reason I was in Oman, so he insisted on taking me to the Amouage perfume factory on the way home to try some of Oman's heavy and exquisite locally made perfume. I have definitely become a perfume snob since discovering frankincense, but Al Ruby persuaded me that this place was the very best and that I should at least take a look. Well, who was I to refuse the firm yet seductive words of Indy?

After lunch, we visited the curious Bimmah Sinkhole, located in Hawiyat Najm Park, literally meaning 'Meteor Fall Park' in Arabic. Some think the hole is a result of a falling meteorite and others that it was created from below. The clear turquoise fresh water at the bottom of this curious hole was very inviting, and Al Ruby and I stood, our hot bodies touching as we admired the view, but time was ticking on and we were in danger of missing opening hours at the perfumery, so off we set on our return journey across the hills listening to an eclectic mix of Bryan Adams, Dido, Zio and Gianna Nannini. Amouage did not disappoint. The perfumes represent Oman in every way for me, mysterious, seductive, elegant, and they stay on your skin, or should I say, they get under your skin? Oman is the perfume capital of Arabia. Roses and sandalwood grow across the region, myrrh is harvested in the valleys close to the Yemeni border, and the world's finest frankincense is tapped from trees in the valleys of Jabal al Qamar, the 'Mountains of the Moon', outside Salalah. Al Ruby and I took every opportunity to smell different scents on each other's bodies, on our wrists, on his manly forearms, on my collarbone, behind our ears. His soft, mid-brown skin was the perfect canvas for these scents, and I was painting a beautiful picture. Was I falling for Oman or falling for the Omani ... maybe a bit of both? On the way home, Al Ruby said he would really like to take me for a drink, but the shy English lass in me reared her ugly head as I explained that I needed to go and pack before my flight that night. A missed opportunity for sure. I should have said yes and taken Indy up on his offer. What harm could one drink do, and a handsome, intelligent man's company should never be declined – note to self!

But my tale of Three Kings did not end there. Who was the third, you may ask? On boarding the plane, I approached my seat to find an older gentleman immaculately dressed in crinkled linen with a face that could tell a thousand tales. Mauro (coincidentally the name of my first Italian boyfriend) turned out to be a retired architect in his sixties who shared his time between Venice and Bali. The Universe was treating me well. Mauro and I proceeded to drink champagne whilst he told me of his life around the world. We laughed as I helped him with his film choices, we ate cheese, drank more champagne, then I fell into a deep sleep. On waking up, Mauro greeted me with a cheery 'Buongiorno' and told me that I looked like an angel whilst sleeping. I was sceptical, imagining myself with my mouth agog and a small amount of dribble escaping, but I thanked him graciously. He said he had enjoyed waking before me and 'tidying our home' and that it was 'a very sweet and romantic imagination'! This man was making me laugh, and I'm sure the other passengers thought we were a couple; the air hostess was definitely addressing us as one. So, when he gave me his number scribbled on a little napkin, I smiled and imagined us sipping prosecco in St Mark's square one day, where his mother used to play the piano. We went through customs together, with Mauro telling the immigration officers that I was his girlfriend! We collected our bags and I kissed him goodbye on his wrinkled, bearded cheeks.

My travels had ended perfectly. A heady mix of culture, adventure, flirting and laughter ... what more could I have asked for? 'We Three Kings' still brings a smile to my face each Christmas as I think of my three handsome encounters. As diverse as gold, frankincense and myrrh and yet each equally precious as the other.

The joy of travelling alone is that you get to meet such characters. I look back and realise that great healing happened during that first transatlantic solo mission. I not only gained confidence in myself but also in mankind. I took myself out of my comfort zone, and my leap of faith paid me back a million times over.

SWEET GOLDEN HONEY LOVE NECTAR

Oman was a supremely extravagant example of self-love. Indulging myself in a treat, just for me. Since my divorce, I had worked on letting go. Letting go of fear, anger, tears, hurt and deception. But I had not worked enough on pulling back in, filling myself back up, refuelling. Oman certainly kick-started that practice for me.

A wonderful Canadian girlfriend explained how I could pull in the 'sweet golden honey love nectar', take it back from those who didn't deserve it, take it from those who offer it and accept all the love gifts until I'm overflowing – so that's exactly what I did. I worked on absorbing that thread of 'sweet golden honey love nectar' and reclaimed it for my own. I imagined myself pulling in a golden thread from above, deep into my body wherever I needed it most. Re-plumping my beating heart, increasing my juiciness, reinstilling my trust and faith so that I was once again totally ready to receive love again. You can do this visualisation practice absolutely anywhere and at any time, in bed, in the car, waiting for the bus, on the loo, even when you are working out. So now, when I see a beautiful woman glowing in a dress that I would love for myself, I don't feel jealous, but instead, I admire her and think, 'Yes, I'd like some of that for myself. I'd like to have that effect on someone else,' and I start visualising that thread.

I am the world's biggest romantic, and every single day, I dream of meeting my soulmate. I imagine travelling the world together, sitting on a train to the Highlands of Scotland with them, trekking together with a backpack on, lying in their arms in a bubble bath and drinking champagne, dancing face to face at my children's weddings and chasing after our grandchildren with this person.

But I have high standards. I need and want to be consumed. I believe that my breath is my spirit. My breath is the wisdom of my heart, my heart's song, which I must listen to. It's not optional. It's a total and absolute obligation. I want my soulmate to breathe it in, to be consumed by it, and to push his spirit into me so that I'm overwhelmed by him, not in an overpowering way but a 'take my breath away' moment, cue Top Gun music and those wafting white curtains!

I want the aching and longing to see this man first thing in the morning and last thing at night. I've had it before ... that passion and deep, deep love. That is what I'm searching for, and I'm not willing to settle for less. So as long as there's a breath in my body, there is hope and a chance that I will find this. He will come to me when the time is perfectly right.

My dream is big yet realistic, and thanks to my gorgeous friend's visualisation practice, I feel so much more worthy.

'You were bewitching and a dangerous piece of work yourself. I'm still 100% sure we've met before ... and before you say it, in this life, rather than a last. Let's go with perilous instead of dangerous. Bewitching, curiously familiar and mellifluous (I had to look that one up!) is a heady and perilous combination. Fortunately (sort of) it's a perilous combination that lives on the other side of the world. Sassy too!' – A message from an encounter of mine that made me feel more than worthy!

'Ignite your highest power, impact and purpose.'

'The flower doesn't dream of the bee.

It blossoms and the bee comes.'

– Mark Nepo

THE QUEEN OF CUPS

I am often asked how I allow myself to love so freely following such heartbreak and deceit. How did I trust again? How have I had years of adventures with such wonderful men and such wonderful friends? Love, for me, encompasses all types of love.

There is no magic formula, and as I said at the beginning of this tale, this book is most definitely not intended as a self-help manual. I see it as a quick read on a sun lounger or take it to the loo. I really am the world's worst reader and for some reason or other, me and a 'how to' or 'self-help' book have never gelled. I can just about cope with an audio version, but even then, it's the author's personal story that always interests me. Those are the bits I remember and that resonate with me. I just love a good, juicy story and can lie in the sun for hours with a gripping tale of intrigue or love. So hopefully, my story will offer some little clues. I really do hope that there might be a little something that gives you the tiniest twinkle in your eye.

Despite the waffle above, having had a long, hard look at the post-apocalypse years, I guess there are a few pointers worth a mention that contributed to my healing and getting back in the saddle, so to speak (wink wink, nudge nudge!). Now I am by no means an expert or professional in these matters. I am not trained in trauma, nor am I a psychologist or coach in any way, shape or form. But sometimes, just living through a similar experience to someone else gives you an understanding and compassion that maybe even the most highly educated and esteemed professional might never quite have.

None of my little ideas below can harm you. Most of them won't cost you a dime. Sometimes simple is good.

Here are my top tips, in no particular order or importance: give yourself time, find love, let it go, cry, practice self-care, write, breathe, spend time in nature, choose, shake, dance, let rip, learn, establish boundaries and be grateful.

Time

Nobody wants to hear this but time, above all, is the greatest healer. Sadly, our impatient, speedy Western society does not favour time. We are all looking for that instant fix which simply doesn't exist. Harsh words but true. Time will soften your wounds, blur your memory and give you space to forgive. It took me a really good five years to feel totally happy, secure with who I am, full of mojo and to have established a compassionate relationship with the father of my kids. I am ten years down the line now, and I can say that I have wholeheartedly forgiven, but I will never forget.

Love

It's ironic, but the one thing you've lost is the one thing you need the most. Love heals everything. It always does. And love comes in so many different forms.

The first and most important thing to do is to make happiness a priority and be gentle with yourself in the process. Mending a broken and bruised heart is a delicate process. Be kind to your heart and start to free it from any past pain. Start slowly and never ever stop, EVER. I still actively work on releasing pain even now because little weeds do grow back and that's OK. It's Mother Nature's natural way. They serve to remind us how incredibly far we have come, how brave we have been and how strong we are. Acknowledge them but trim them back regularly with compassion. Maybe that sounds a bit 'weewa, woowa', so below, I've made a list of practical activities I do from time to time to help myself trim. I love a regular trim and yes, I know where your mind is wandering to if you're anything like me! Attending to your 'lady or gentleman garden', if that is something you like to do, can also be a very therapeutic form of self-love.

Can I suggest you listen to Katy Perry's version of the classic, 'All You Need is Love'?

Fantastic ways to release pain:

- Shamanic fire ceremony
- Qoya lesson (www.sonjalockyer.com)
- Journaling
- Ecstatic Dance
- Sacred Scroll writing (www.ElisabetAlfstad.com)
- Shaking
- Dancing
- Tapping (www.rapidtapping.com)
- Grounding or walking barefoot in nature

When I was in Bali, I wrote an email about love – on Valentine's Day, in fact – that I'd like to share here. For me, it highlights one of the most important forms of love – self-love.

Love, Actually

Happy Valentine's Day to you all, my beautiful tribe.

I may not have a conventional 'love' in my life today, but boy oh boy do I have love all around me, and so the feeling goes ... cue Billy Mack from *Love, Actually*. A love-fest, in fact!

I woke up to an amazing photo of my 106-year-old Nan with an alpaca that had come to visit the home where she is. In fact, two alpacas, in the middle of the lounge, surrounded by inquisitive old faces. I do wonder what they made of each other. The smile that beamed on my face was enormous and set the tone for the day.

Today is the seventh anniversary of my operation when a level 4 ulcerated melanoma was removed from my back. The person I needed most left my bedside that day in a London hospital, and I'm pretty sure checked out of our relationship at that moment too. What followed was a sad, blurry, devastating few years dealing with fear, heartbreak and the realisation that life would never be the same again.

So it's a biggie for me today because my lucky number is seven. I am born on the seventh, along with my epic twin sis, and there have always been sevens in my life.

To honour this, I fasted for seven days, finishing today when I broke fast and was blessed in a closing ceremony by a Balinese high priest and priestess. I threw away all that I no longer want and welcomed in more adventure, more discoveries, more travels and above all, even more LOVE, and on Valentine's Day of all days!

I love Valentine's Day and don't find it corny one iota. You don't have to buy into all the commercialism, but how important is it to make a point of feeling love, giving love and receiving love, and if that's what this day brings, then AHO!

Life has turned into the most incredibly beautiful, authentic, revealing, hilarious and fun-filled adventure. I am the strongest, happiest and healthiest I have ever been. I'm living in beautiful Bali, where my body, mind and soul are being nourished and loved beyond my wildest dreams. I have the space to spend amazing amounts of time with my children whilst they still want to hang with their mum. I love the simplicity of life. I love the ocean. I love the heat. I love the blue skies. I love the crazy rain. I love writing. I love all the interesting people I meet from all over the world. I love school and its community. My kids love their school more than anything. There really is a magic to this place that I find tricky to put into words, but it's like Bali snaps you out of old habits. Every day there's a new adventure, a new encounter, a new challenge. A five-minute chat with a stranger can seem like an incredible five-hour discussion. You also have the privilege of time, which for me means I think a lot about why I am here and how best I can serve this world. Not why I'm here in Bali, but why am I here on this Earth? I think I'm here to love, to encourage love, to spread love. To be love's biggest cheerleader.

So today, for me, is all about self-love. Loving my body with its big scar and the fact that it survived a pretty horrible trauma and healed and supported me through my emotional ups and downs. I am giving my body all the love I can.

I'm preparing a Valentine's feast for myself and the bambinos. Not exactly post-fast protocol (ssshhhhhh), but it feels like the right thing to do. I have a table full of deliciousness, and I just can't wait!

Until teatime, I am writing, which you know I love. Writing for myself and writing for you, of course. I love when you write back to me. I love that I can still connect with you all … an incredibly lovely community from all journeys of my life.

So as I sign off, I want to say thank you for all the love you give and send you all the love imaginable from the heart of my very cleansed bottom (14 coffee-and-garlic enemas later and it's as pure as the driven snow!).

Big Bali Love to my kids, my tribe of angels, my family, my friends, my lovers and my past loves.

Let it Go! (cue Elsa in Frozen)

Pain is of no service whatsoever, I promise. It won't change what happened. It won't enable payback. What it will do is harm YOU. It could even make you poorly. I suggest you symbolically wrap it up in a big bundle and chuck it out to sea or down a flowing river, or plant it deep within the earth. Mother Nature loves our pain. She takes it deep down within her and transforms it into the most nourishing compost, so give freely and often. You can either visualise this entire process in your head or, even better, find a large substantial rock, pour your pain into it and throw it away (or plant it) with the biggest, deepest, bone-shaking scream or moan from the depths of your belly. This is exactly what I did at a shamanic retreat in Normandy many, many years ago and it felt so good. It was liberating and made me sob like never before, releasing even more pain.

Cry

Talking of tears, cry. I cried every single night for a whole year when my ex-husband left me. Let the tears flow because they help to cleanse you. If you feel like you want to cry, let yourself cry because I see it as your body's way of wanting to release the anguish or stress. Plus, don't be scared to cry with people or on people, your loved ones or even an acquaintance. The English culture isn't great at showing its feelings … stiff upper lip and all that, but it's just so unhealthy. If you've been hurt, then it's fine to show it and never feel guilty. Did you know that the word cry comes from the Latin 'quiritare', which means 'raise a public outcry', literally 'call on the Quirites (Roman citizens) for help'? Our tears are a cry for help, so let yourself receive that help, that hug, that tissue. Think of crying as letting off that flare. It's your signal that you are in need of compassion; otherwise, how are people to know? You'll see that, slowly, your tears will flow less freely and less frequently, and you'll feel some healing.

Self-Care

Radical self-care is vital. I had cancer on my side. That feels like a weird thing to say but it's totally true. My diagnosis meant that I actually had to look after myself really well. I had two small bambinos, and there was absolutely no way that they were growing up without their mummy. I knew that if I let myself get overly stressed or angry or distraught, this would only exacerbate my cancer. Now I am definitely not wishing cancer on anyone, but you can choose to look after yourself and your own survival. Put your experience

into perspective. Be empowered and brave and look after yourself, mind, body and soul. Eat well, exercise and get professional help. Choose who you surround yourself with and get up every morning, put one foot in front of the other, smile (even if it's a tiny one), and you will always find something to be grateful for.

My self-care mainly takes place first thing with my morning rituals which I've listed below. I don't necessarily complete them all every day, but some days I do, and that's when my energy is zingy, I have a brighter twinkle in my eye, and my smile smiles even bigger than normal. My writings will flow with ease, my conversations will be that little bit more insightful. It's like my self-investment comes right back at me with a healthy dose of interest.

- The Wellbeing Morning Ritual Club with a soul sister of mine (www.sonjalockyer.com).

- 30-day yoga programmes with Adriene on YouTube.

- HIIT sessions, spinning sessions, anything that gets me super sweaty, super quickly.

- Tibetan 5 exercises.

- Pulling an oracle/angel card. My favourite packs are:
  - o *Wild Kuan Yin Oracle* by Alana Fairchild
  - o *Work Your Light* by Rebecca Campbell
  - o *Practical Magic* by Kate Taylor
  - o *Rumi Oracle* by Alana Fairchild
  - o *Lemurian Starchild Oracle* by Leanne Carpenter & Michiel Kroon
  - o *The Starchild Tarot* by Danielle Noel

- Journaling or writing Morning Pages, one of the most effective tools for cultivating creativity, personal growth, and change, from *The Artist's Way* by Julia Cameron.

- Super greens powders - I've tried so many types and they mainly taste like pond water, but I'm addicted to a pint a day.

- A mid-morning, steamy, frothy chaga cappuccino with homemade almond milk (see the recipe below) or a bulletproof coffee with butter and MCT oil. I also add lion's mane (a type of mushroom which you can get as a powder) to my coffee to try to help protect against dementia.

- A walk by the ocean, a swim in the sea, a quick dip in the river, a plunge in the pool or a cold shower.

- A post-lunch mug of matcha tea for that necessary pick-me-up.

- Painted toenails always.

- Bake. For me, there is something wonderfully grounding, homely and rewarding about baking, and you'll find a favourite recipe of mine below: that all-time favourite, banana bread!

- And why not end your day (not every day, but once or twice, perhaps) with a final treat, a glow-inducing gin & tonic (with or without alcohol). My all-time favourite is the rosemary and butterfly pea G&T at Hujan Local restaurant in Ubud, Bali. If not a G&T, then a mug of magnesium powder aids me in a peaceful night's sleep.

Homemade Almond Chaga Cappuccino

Soak around three handfuls of almonds in water in the fridge overnight. The next morning, rinse, then blitz them really well in a powerful blender with two pitted dates, a pinch of really good salt and some fresh water. Then strain through a nut bag by squeezing out the milk. The result is a silky, decadent, alabaster liquid that froths like a dream. To elevate my coffee a step further, I add a sprinkling of ceremonial cacao and a quarter teaspoon of chaga mushroom extract.

Chaga mushroom extract is often referred to as a precious gift from nature. It is grown on a variety of species of trees, particularly birch, with which it has a symbiotic relationship helping to heal it. For centuries people have used this nutrient-rich, dense powder to balance chi, boost the immune system and promote good health in general. I love it added to my coffee because it stops me from getting the jitters from the caffeine. And if you can double the quantity and share a cup with a friend, that's even better.

Cinnamon & Ginger Banana Bread

This wonderfully earthy vegan banana bread recipe by Melissa Hemsley is incredibly nourishing, especially toasted and slathered with some salty nut butter on a chilly afternoon.

Ingredients:
300g flour
4 medium to large ripe bananas
1 tbsp ground cinnamon
1 tbsp ground ginger
Pinch of salt
3 tsp baking powder
1 tsp lemon juice
60 ml melted coconut oil
2 tbsp maple syrup
200 ml water
Small handful of pitted dates, roughly chopped

1. Preheat the oven to 190 degrees C and in a large bowl, combine the flour, baking powder, cinnamon, ginger and salt before adding the lemon juice and stirring gently.

2. Add the water, maple syrup and coconut oil.

3. Mash three of the bananas (saving the fourth for cutting into coins and laying on top) and add to the flour mix, then stir through the dates.

4. Line a loaf tin with baking paper, pour in the mix, top with the banana coins and bake for 50 minutes until firm, golden and cooked throughout. You can check with a skewer if it comes out clean.

5. I sometimes add shards of chocolate into the loaf before cooking for an extra mouthful of gooey indulgence, and of course, you could use vegan chocolate.

Write

I mentioned journaling before, and I remember my Fairy Godmother, at our very first session all those years ago, saying to me, 'Just write.' I didn't get it, which sounds ridiculous as I'd written all my life for my various jobs, but I had never kept a diary or journal. It took me many, many months, and then finally, one day, I sat down and started writing. The effect was instant and incredible. I couldn't stop. I didn't care what I was writing about, whether it made sense, if there were spelling mistakes, I just poured all that was in my mind onto the pages, and since then, I have rarely stopped and here's why. I wrote this email at the start of my second year in Bali, and reading it now, it sums up perfectly why I simply have to write. And when I got the wobbles about publishing this book, which happened to me on almost a daily basis for years, I remind myself that I know one thing for sure and that is that I want to own my story. People need to learn from your failures and people need to learn from your successes, and that is what drives me to share this, even if it is uncomfortable.

Ma Joie de Vivre, Ma Joie d'Ecrire
(My joy of life, my joy of writing)

From landing back in Bali at the end of January, I've had a significant few months of 'deep diving' and figuring out a load of shit which can really all be summarised in one word – BOUNDARIES!

Beautiful but raw Bali got me well and truly by the short 'n curlies. It made me delve deeper than ever before to the very murky depths of my soul. It stripped me bare of my 'Englishness' and my Libran traits of trying to keep everything lovely and rosy. It wasn't particularly comfortable. It was certainly unexpected, but I got spat out the other side with the shield that was around my heart relocated to my solar plexus, feeling fully embodied in my inner power and my lioness walking proud in all her sweaty, frizzy haired glory.

I received enough acoustic bio-resonance sound healing to vibrate every cell of my body to the point it might think I was raving in front of a whopping speaker in Pacha, Ibiza.

The pillows and bolsters at Pyramids of Chi (a sound healing centre) had been thrashed to within an inch of their lives during Dynamic Meditation. Instead of being 'terribly PC' as one used to, I screamed and yelled and sobbed out those sneaky feelings that get burrowed deep into the dark and dingy parts of your body. It was like necking a shedload of Heineken and refreshing parts that other beers couldn't reach!

Biodynamic Craniosacral Therapy with a delicious alpha male left my solar plexus full of fire. Sacred women's circles with my tribe and sessions with my inimitable Fairy Godmother fuelled me with love and laughter.

Finally, the most excruciatingly, unexpectedly scary workshop exploring my Soul Constellations was the last straw. I could have puked all over that yoga studio and run for the rice paddies, but that's a whole book in itself. After years of 'work', this felt like the raw, naked, gritty icing on the cake.

So come April, I was done. No more diving. (I do love a spot of snorkelling, though!) No more healing. I just wanted to play, and play I did. I had a wonderful couple of free weeks whilst my kid's dad was here. I travelled, I played, I frolicked and I wrote, but then 'pop' went my bubble. I received some feedback from my last email to you all that made me feel uneasy about writing for the first time ever. Well, that's an understatement, actually. It stopped me dead in my tracks, and I honestly considered never writing again.

I wrote one line about the father of my children. It took me seven years to pluck up the courage to write that down on paper. I felt it was relevant to the rest of my email. I didn't write that line to cause hurt or point blame. I wrote it to speak my truth, to put my feelings and email into context. So when I found out that a 'mutual friend' of mine and my kids' father had sent it to him with an alarmed comment, I felt sick to the bottom of my Bali belly.

And then I became intrigued. Do I write for approval? No. I write because it brings me to life. It's my mojo. It makes me tick. And yes,

I like to stay in touch with people. So why did this incident affect me so much? I'm the one that put that sentence out there, so I should be prepared for any feedback, shouldn't I? But interestingly, it left me feeling betrayed and saddened. I came to the conclusion that if I'd been writing about someone else, I would have defended what I'd written without a second thought. It wouldn't have touched the sides. However, this involved me and someone incredibly important in my life who I have worked really hard with to respect and behave with dignity around.

Then, the other evening I clicked on Brené Brown: The Call to Courage on Netflix, which if any of you know Brené, was the perfect kick up my arse! Two of her famous quotes resounded within me like Big Ben's bells …

'I want to be in the arena. I want to be brave with my life. And when we make the choice to dare greatly, we sign up to get our asses kicked. We can choose courage or we can choose comfort, but we can't have both. Not at the same time.'

'You either walk inside your story and own it or you stand outside your story and hustle for your worthiness.'

Never a truer word said Brené. I do want to be brave enough to write my story, but I can only tell it from my perspective, and I guess that's going to potentially upset some people. Do I feel really, truly comfortable with that? Not really if I'm honest … so there I was, stumped again!

****

Fast forward to July, and the past couple of weeks have been spent in France, reconnecting with lots of dear friends. More than one has asked me why I stopped writing and asked me to start again, including my Fairy Godmother (aka my coach, therapist, general worker of magic), who, rather than 'asked', pinned me in the corner of a party and made me pinky promise that by next year my book would be completed and she told me how! Like waving a magic wand over me, I now know how to finish writing the book. The woman is a genius. So whoopee and yikes! Now you can all hold me accountable, and please feel free to kick me up the proverbial at any time, just like Brené did.

I have decided to choose courage over comfort, which for me means being vulnerable, not something this 46-year-old, fiercely independent woman tapping away on her keyboard is particularly good at. But I know I've been brave in the past, and this is a walk in the park in comparison. If I fail, I fail, but at least I've tried.

So there we go, like nothing happened, I'm back at my ancient old laptop. Tapping away with the biggest smile on my face and butterflies in my stomach. Ready and excited to press SEND again. I'm walking inside my story and I'm owning it, sister!

I'm glad, in a way, that I had this time of reflection, but I'm so ready to keep growing which simply means writing for me. It floats my boat and I need that boat well and truly afloat to keep journeying through this wonderful life of mine and this incredible world. My boat ain't done sailing yet … it's got a long way to go.

Breathe

Learn to breathe again from deep down in your belly. Take deep healing belly breaths that will nourish your cells. When we are stressed, we breathe from high up in our chests in a shallow fashion that keeps us alive, but it doesn't restore us. Breathe in the peace and exhale the stress. My two breath gurus are Sonja Lockyer (@sonjalockyer on Instagram) and Wim Hof (@iceman_hof). They will teach you everything you ever need to know about the incredible restorative gift of breath. It's mind-blowing stuff and yet so simple, so accessible and totally free ... 'the most beautiful jewel, never bought, never sold.'* A complete and utter game-changer.

*Imelda May

Nature

Get into nature. Mother Nature is the greatest healer. Being outside, even standing barefoot on a small piece of grass, will help you to ground and to regain your foothold on this planet, which is either temporarily lost or altered when we experience heartbreak.

If you were anything like me, you just wanted to retreat from everything, to hide away, cover your ears and deal with the pain in complete privacy. Other than my children, I would have been happy to have lived totally alone. Being in nature will revive your sense of spirit and your desire to tread among the living again. So, take your shoes off and try it, just for a few quiet moments.

121

Choose

Always remember that it is your choice to decide if a painful event is going to stop you – maybe for a while, maybe forever – from moving forward with a smile on your face or if you are going to learn from it. You have incredible power, you are an individual, and your partner's actions are theirs, not yours. Remind yourself constantly that what happened is a reflection of them and not of you. This never has to happen to you again. You didn't cause it. Find your faith. The world is chock-full of wonderful people. Gorgeous, generous, kind, loving folk that are out there waiting to meet you. If you think you're going to meet a weirdo, you'll most probably meet a weirdo, so don't think it because you'll attract it! Feel how you want to feel again. Imagine a time and a place when you were so happy, when you felt amazing in your body and when your surroundings were divine. Use that feeling to remind your soul how it can feel. I love doing this practice. I can literally feel a wave of warmth surge up through my body ending in a huge smile. You have the power, I promise you. I am a huge fan of rapid tapping, and my guru, Poppy Delbridge (@rapidtapping), has taught me how to tap to release and clear, then how to tap to manifest. It's a simple yet powerful process that helps you to realise your power and potential. The results are mind-blowing and will quite possibly be the subject of my second book!

Shake

If you've never shaken before, you're missing a trick. I first discovered shaking during a Qoya class and it was a revelation. I'm going to tell you a little story now about a gazelle.

Once upon a time, there was a gazelle casually grazing in the African savanna, whiling away the day without a care in the world. Then suddenly, a lion appeared out of nowhere and started chasing the poor gazelle. Now the gazelle was speedy but so was the lion, and the chase was intense. Finally, the gazelle got away. She was pretty traumatised, to say the least, as you would be when your life nearly comes to an end. However, the gazelle did not book in for therapy or reach into the medicine cabinet for a pill. Instead, the gazelle shook. She shook and shook and shook. She shook all that trauma right out of her little body and went back to her grazing.

Psychologists the world over have noticed that prey animals like deer and gazelles are constantly under threat of dying but they show no symptoms of trauma. The process of shaking is the animal's instinctive way of releasing the event. It's incredibly clever yet oh so simple, and we humans can do the same, but it's not something we're ever really shown or taught unless you are part of a shamanic community.

Start by holding your arms out in front of you and shaking one hand really quickly. Then stop and feel the difference. It will feel like the hand and arm you shook is alive, like it is buzzing, like your cells are having a party. Now go through the whole of your body from your feet to your head. You can even lie down on your back and shake your extremities like a little bug. You can make noises. Don't think about what you're doing. Just let that trauma come out of your mouth. I bet your bottom dollar that you'll feel a tiny bit better.

'Trauma is a fact of life. It does not, however, have to be a life sentence.'

– Dr Peter Levine, PhD
Founder of Somatic Experiencing

Dance

Get yourself into a space, no matter how large or small. Find that tune that makes you smile, that gets your feet tapping or your shoulders jigging. Turn it up to full volume and DANCE YOUR SEXY ASS OFF, PEOPLE! As the delectable Matthew McConaughey says, 'Don't half-ass it.' Give it your all and don't give a damn about what you look like, just dance, dance, dance! You might even want to grab yourself a wooden spoon or hairbrush and do some lip synching too.

Here are a few goodies to get you started if you need some inspiration. An eclectic mix, if I do say so myself!

- 'Feeling Good' by Michael Buble – this has to be my all-time favourite. I can literally see my kids' eyes rolling in their heads as I write this!
- 'Titanium' by David Guetta and Sia
- 'Don't Stop Me Now' by Queen
- 'Burn' by Ellie Goulding
- 'I'm Unstoppable' by Sia
- 'Be the One' by Dua Lipa
- 'Shake It Out' by Florence + The Machine
- 'Crazy in Love' by Beyonce and JAY-Z
- 'Something Better' by Tom Grennan
- 'Jerusalema' by Master KG (and learn the routine, it's so much fun!)
- 'Now We Are Free' by Lisa Gerrard
- 'Warrior' by Aurora
- 'All You Need is Love' by the Beatles but sung by Katy Perry
- 'Don't Stop the Music' by Rihanna ... such great advice, Rihanna

Let Rip

Yep, you heard me! Every now and again, simply let your hair down, lose your self-control and have a mahoosive blowout. This might not be the most PC advice I can give you, but sometimes you just need to shake things up. I go for it once or twice a year. I feel the build-up and boom, all hell breaks loose and it feels bloody marvellous. Honestly, it works a treat as a reset and a reminder that sometimes we just hold it together too much, so let it all go. Go wild, be free and just 'blow the bloody wheels off'! Here's an account of just such an occurrence.

Big Summer Blowout!

Holy moly guacamole, did I have a blowout on Saturday! It occurred to me not to share this shameful, rather out-of-character episode with all you lovely people. I mean, I'm supposed to be all zen and cleansed and respecting my mind and body in Bali, aren't I? Then I thought about it again and I want my writing to be honest. Plus, I know I'm not the only mum or dad who feels the need to let rip from time to time ... although there's a blowout and there's a Bali blowout!

The peaceful, civilised evening I had planned consisted of a heart-warming movie at the wonderfully chilled vegan cinema where we could indulge in kombucha and sushi followed by maybe one drink before returning to my new babysitter, who had imposed a curfew on me!

Jeez, sister, holy crap, OMG and WTF ... well, that didn't go to plan!

I messed up and read the wrong movie and instead, we arrived to find out there was a horror film being shown. On watching the trailer that the very kind lady on reception showed us, my shrieks of fear and violent, jerky body movements made it clear that this wasn't going to be an option, so onto Plan B.

Turning right out of the cinema, we immediately found ourselves in a seriously cool bar with seriously delicious cocktails that were just too enticing to say no to. One turned to two which turned to three, by which point all thoughts of dinner, responsibility and duty had left my merry head. We promptly moved on to another bar, ironically called No Mas, which means 'No More' in Bahasa Indonesian. Well, the message clearly didn't reach me and the DJ's super cheesy tunes were too much to resist. Up I got with my umpteenth margarita in hand and hit that dance floor. I was also totally elated to meet an adorable Welsh couple, Hannah and Rodrey, who quickly became partners in crime and we danced the night away, fuelled with litres of tequila and laughter.

Needless to say, I don't remember leaving the bar or getting home. My next 'compos mentis' moment was waking up, fully clothed, in-between the kiddies with my son asking me in a very confused little voice why on earth I was in bed with them, fully dressed and snoring like a wounded warthog. Ohhhh, deary me – BAD MUMMY MOMENT OR WHAT?!

I can honestly say I experienced my worst hangover for years and years. I could barely get vertical, and the kids had to fend for themselves, which they are more than capable of, but the guilt I felt was awful. My son was so concerned that I was sharing a glass of water with my daughter as he thought I was contagious until my

daughter, with an evil snigger, pointed out that I wasn't sick, just incredibly hungover. Thanks, love!

The icing on the cake came when we were at the school bus stop on Monday morning, and I met a lovely new couple who were popping their sweet little girl on the bus for the first time. My boy boldly announced at full volume that 'Mummy was so hungover yesterday that we had had to go to the pizza shop alone to get takeaway for dinner.' Oh, the shame of it!!!! Nothing like having your dirty laundry aired in public to new acquaintances.

So where did this little outburst come from, I ask myself?

I'd been feeling rather odd last week, grumpy and stuck, and I had no idea why. It certainly has been a crazy few weeks. Getting back to school with all the meetings, arranging activities, new parents, new friends, and I feel like I've been making a whole load of decisions. I know it's my choice to bring the children here on my own without family nearby for support, but that also means I'm fully responsible for them on my own, night and day. I think the mummy duties had got the better of me.

It was like a hurricane of unrest swirling around inside of me, and I guess it just went tornado-style on Saturday night and ripped through Ubud and my liver in one almighty twister.

Do I regret it? Not one bit. I think I needed that blowout to reset myself. I think we all do from time to time, and I have decided not to hold onto the guilt or shame. I rolled out my yoga mat yesterday and it felt amazing. The view from my little home looks like it's gone into super-duper technicolour, and the green juice I devoured tasted better than ever.

And to finish this email off, I have to share an extremely precious moment. My son came home from school last night, obviously concerned that his useless mum was back up and running and kindly asked me, 'So Mummy, are you overhung now?'. I howled with laughter and from this day on, when I am over my hangovers, I will refer to myself as being 'overhung'!

With love, shame, laughter and an affirmative 'aho, you only live once' from moi xxx

aka Beyoncé, Madonna, Britney (oh yeah baby, I strutted my stuff to the lot!) and finally Cindy Lauper because Girls Just Wanna Have Fun!

Learn

The human brain is an enigma to me. Our capacity to learn and never stop learning is mind-blowing. I learn best from other people, from travel and, funnily enough, from writing things down or saying them out loud. When we learn about others, we learn about ourselves, the biggest gift of all.

'Live as if you were to die tomorrow.
Learn as if you were to live forever.'

– Mahatma Gandhi

Here's an email that I wrote about learning and that makes me yearn to travel again as it forces you to learn. I'm getting itchy feet for sure! It also reminds me that I am in control, no one else! I am the only person in control of my life.

Keep Learning

Today I started the day with the intention of writing all day. The distractions in Bali are abundant and tempting, but I know that writing is my nirvana. I spend a lot of time feeling guilty about not writing and I've finally figured out why. It's my body's way of reminding me how much good it does me, and if I didn't feel those twinges, then maybe I would just forget and never write again.

The day started with quite a strong aftershock, jars wobbling in the kitchen, which was a first but something we are getting used to. Then a poorly boy home from school. I got the time wrong for Pilates so ended up dashing down the road like a wild banshee. I was all-a-fluster, a very Sweaty Betty, but as I lay down on the transformer just in time, I thought, 'Good Golly Miss Molly, that's been a rather bumpy start to the day!' So I took a moment and decided to restart. I didn't want the day to continue like that, and it was up to me to change it.

I got home and restarted my day on Bali time, cooking my porridge slowly with love and making it extra special with loads of flaxseed, ground almonds and walnuts, bee pollen, coconut sugar and bananas. I wanted to nourish my writing and also my poorly boy. It was so much more delicious and enjoyable to eat, and I felt set up for the day ahead.

This is one of the most important things I have learnt in the last few years – that we are in control of how our day goes. It's totally up to us, even with outside influences, how to deal with them and how they affect us. We are our own bosses – no one else.

It was also a wonderful reminder to slow down. I needed to come back to Bali time and function at half speed which this wondrous place allows you the rare opportunity to do.

The trembling aftershock was also a reminder of the power of Mother Earth. She's having a rough time right now, and we feel aftershocks daily and nightly most days. We have only ended up under the kitchen table once, and I would say the feeling is more intrigue than fear so far. Compared to what the poor people in Lombok are experiencing, this is a gentle fairground ride, so we need to relax. My lovely son made me smile last week as there was quite a major aftershock one lunchtime, so when the kids came home, I asked them if they had felt it at school. They were both so relaxed about the whole thing and my son's reply was, 'Oh, Mummy, it was just so annoying. We were in the middle of the most amazing mindfulness and we had to go outside.' That was music to my ears and made me realise that a) this is definitely where we should be for now and b) that there's no point getting fearful of what might happen. We are very aware of the suffering that is happening in Lombok and are supporting all the wonderful fundraising going on around us, and that is how we can help right now. We are curious as to why there are so many quakes but it is out of our control, so there is no point waking up each day in fear of what might or might not happen.

I actually started this email back in June, but it never felt complete. However, coming back to Bali has reminded me of all the things I have learnt here and am continuing to learn, which is the reason I love to travel so much – it forces you to learn.

You observe a new culture, the way things are done, you learn a new language, you meet new people who always teach you new things if you are open and receptive to it. You learn that actually, home is no matter where you are with your children or loved ones. It's not the bricks and mortar full of belongings.

You see how other cultures do things and realise that your way is no better than theirs, it's simply different. It puts things into perspective. Does it really matter if your bin is full to bursting with large ants? Not really, it's a bin! Is it the end of the world to come back to mouldy cupboards, a dead bird on the doorstep and a dead mouse down the road? Nope! I learnt it's better just to get on and deal with such things rather than get upset and waste time complaining to the landlord who lives in Japan and has no control over the situation. Wiping out the cupboards with the wonderful Thieves (an essential oil blend) to prevent mould had to be done anyway, and I think I could probably deal with nuclear fallout with the rubber glove, paper bag, kitchen roll, bin bag concoction I invented to pick up the dead birdy!

Before the summer holidays, I spent two afternoons at school listening to the Middle School Quest Presentations and the High School Greenstone Presentations, which are like TED talks that the kids do to graduate. I was utterly blown away by the honesty, depth, creativity, passion and drive of these kids. There was an amazing array of subjects covered and projects undertaken, from installing Lo-Fi into Green School by a 14-year-old, to talking about ADHD, to creating a machine that harnesses the force of waves to create power ... the list was endless. We're not talking anything vaguely wishy-washy – these are subjects and projects that many adults would have a tough time undertaking.

We were on our feet time after time after time with standing ovations, tears in our eyes and covered in goosebumps, but the talk that hit me the most was a High School Graduate who had suffered with mental health issues, including panic attacks and depression, from a young age. She wrote beautiful, powerful poetry, which she shared with us and spoke about how writing was a real saviour for her – something I can identify with. She asked us all to write, but to be totally truthful and honest ... to literally spill our thoughts onto paper, empty our feelings into the open and see how it felt.

I have really tried to take this on board with writing my book. It's a bit scary as I was so private about so much at the time, but I want it to be an honest and truthful tale of part of my life and how I experienced the pure violence of being abandoned by the person I needed most when I thought I was going to die. I have to be brave enough to just be me and tell it how it was, whether this upsets people or not.

Many of the kids talked about how Green School let them be themselves, be honest with who they were and not who they thought they should be to fit in. Another incredibly powerful lesson. If I'm honest, I've spent quite a part of my adult life not feeling like I fit in. I can feel awkward in social situations. I don't know whether it's not having another half in the room as backup, being a single mum or not wanting to impose on people? Maybe it's just me and my funny ways? I know I have many! I've never been able to put my finger on it. Invite me to an adult party on my own and I am filled with complete and utter dread. I never really know how to chit chat to people, and I long to be one of the social butterflies you see drifting from one new introduction to the other, at ease with themselves and always with something interesting to say. Is it not working that makes me feel awkward? I mean, I earn good money, but I don't work a 9-5. I also feel like the odd one out in my immediate family. They are all so 'settled'. Home has always been where I am with the kiddies, but I also long to find that place in the world where I feel I belong. Then I picked this oracle card … does this explain it all?

From the *Work Your Light Oracle Cards* by Rebecca Campbell

MINTAKAN – Longing for home. Belonging. The original Lightworkers.

Many Mintakans have an odd longing for 'home' and struggle with feeling like they don't belong. It is thought that this is due to their home planet no longer being in existence. If you pulled this card, it could mean that you are a Mintakan or are longing for a sense of belonging and root chakra healing is necessary for you to feel secure and safe.

Perhaps you feel this longing to find home without knowing where that is. Perhaps you've been moving around a lot and yearn for a place on Earth to call your own. If so, you are being called to connect with Mother Earth and create it for yourself now. To choose where you feel most at home and create it, rather than waiting for the feeling of belonging to come.

So where is my True North? Where do I feel most at home? It definitely was France for a long while. Will it be England? I guess the only way is to give it a go and see. Maybe I will end up in the beautiful Cap Ferret on the West coast of France one day, where my soul sings. Maybe I will be able to juggle a life between two places that I love? I'm impatient in a way, but at the same time, it's a wonderfully exciting journey figuring it out!

I realise this is rather an eclectic email, but at the end of the day, it all comes back to learning which I am enthusiastically committed to doing for the rest of my life. So if you ever come across me and I'm being close-minded, too judgemental or can't be bothered to listen, I give you full permission to slap me across the face with a Thieves-infused wet flannel, a nuclear fallout rubber glove or simply look me in the eye and remind me of this email.

Until the next time … all my love, Miss Molly Mintakan

Boundaries

I am certainly not the oracle or the expert on this subject. In fact, it has taken me ten whole years to finally establish healthy, balanced boundaries and it's been really tricky. My kids were tiny when their dad and I split up, and they're still kids today, living at home with me, so we have to communicate about them. However, I allowed that communication to become too familiar. I allowed him to remain too much in my life, and I admit that over the years, I allowed those boundaries to become blurred. I was too accommodating, too willing to pick up the slack or fill in where necessary and it didn't do me any favours. I would do anything for my kids, but I'm not just their mum, and I am my ex-husband's ex-wife, not his first wife still. He chose to leave and therefore, it was his decision to leave that part of his life behind.

I was on a two-week medical retreat in Italy last year. It was an extremely indulgent early 50th birthday gift to myself and I don't regret it one iota. It was day one and I was sitting on one of those really posh outdoor sofas in my white fluffy robe, sipping my morning juice, when a lady came up and sat next to me. Within moments she'd extracted my life story from me and then told me the following in the most straightforward way. 'How on earth was the Universe going to supply me with a soulmate because, as far as it was concerned, that part of life was still filled by my ex-husband!' It was one of those brief moments that changed my life forever. I needed to create a chasm, a void from him.

I realised that I existed in a co-dependency with him. He financially supported us, and therefore I felt I owed him. I felt I was still somehow responsible for his wellbeing, but that most certainly is not my job. He never demanded that of me. It was something I gave freely, but it was so unhealthy.

At that very moment in Italy, I decided that enough was enough. I was done. Basta, finito, no more! I spent the summer actively and intently recreating my boundaries. Ironically, my summer plans were turned on their head and I ended up spending more time than ever with my ex-husband. He was kind and generous with me. It felt like a summer of firsts and lasts. Staying in his incredible home. We even went on a luxurious family holiday. For the first time in forever, I felt myself saying, 'fuck it'. It was kind of like an experiment. I was extremely grateful and it should have felt fantastic, but instead, it felt frivolous. I disconnected from my soul and it left me feeling empty – grateful, yes, but empty. But it was a process I needed to go through, the very last few miles of my ten-year-long journey that I had to walk.

Amazingly, big shifts happened and it really was all down to the lady on that posh sofa! I genuinely feel able and, more importantly, incredibly willing to put myself first. My ex reacted badly at first to my new, strong boundaries, calling me passive-aggressive, and I get that. I changed and it took him a while to understand what I was doing, but now it just feels fantastic between us. Our communication only involves our kids. It is kept to a bare minimum and is respectful and caring.

I was not in a safe place with my boundaries and that is what I crave most in my heart. Those six little letters – SAFETY – are the most important thing for me in all areas of my life, my home life, my kid's life and, of course, my romantic life. I want to be able to rely on someone to have my back. It's all about how I want to feel and not what I want to do.

Be Grateful

Finally, and this will take time, be grateful. Everything happens for a reason. My experience with my ex-husband cracked me open so wide that my heart, guts and spirit were spilt all over my beautiful wooden parquet floor. Yes, I can laugh now, but I couldn't back then. I had to rebuild myself entirely and that process allowed me to become the best ever version of myself; to live by my values; to spend time with the people who truly nourish me; to be fully responsible for my actions; to make my own decisions and to be the most glorious version of 'me' I could imagine. I live every day with optimism and excitement and pride in myself for what I have accomplished and for who I am now. I love myself and I love my life.

YOUR VIBE ATTRACTS
YOUR TRIBE

As my tale draws to an end for now, I would like to tell you about my tribe because, quite frankly, finding your people (oh my word, that sounds cheesy!) is essential in life. This is the last piece of advice that I have no qualms about offering up.

'When you find people who not only tolerate your quirks but celebrate them with cries of "me too!" be sure to cherish them because those weirdos are your tribe.'

– AJ Downey

They've held me at my lowest and soared with me at my highest. Several camps or groups have emerged over the years, forming my pyramid of support, love and laughter, with my blood family at the heart and my two children at the bottom.

My kids are the foundation of my very being, but with that, I put no responsibility upon them. Being a mother whilst trying to repair yourself physically, mentally and emotionally was the hardest thing to take on, but at the same time, they provided me with the focus and drive to carry on each day. They kept me busy, balanced and entertained. I simply would not be the woman I am without them in my world.

'Live so that when your children think of love, truth and integrity, they think of you.'

– @kundalinigown

My darling hearts, my two children, who I wholeheartedly believe chose me to be their mummy and to teach me daily.

My daughter is the masculine energy in my life and I often refer to her as a 'force to be reckoned with'. Yep, she'd give Darth Vader a run for his money. She is here to remind me to put myself first sometimes, maybe often, without shame. Born with little, if no fear, she has a hunger for the world. She's no pushover. She wasn't even bothered by her traumatic, 'touch n go' birth. One small cry and a paracetamol for her broken collarbone were all she needed. A wise Yoda with a Bridget Bardot hairstyle and sassiness that she is unaware of right now, but it won't be long. I see the boys looking at that honey hair, at that stunning figure, and I know she'll tread many of the paths I have walked but for sure with much less self-doubt and self-deprecation. She is 'the incredible', a name she gave herself and a name she lives by.

My son was born two years later to the day, and he is the human incarnation of an angel. Physically, mentally and spiritually, he is the real-life embodiment of a cherub with an unearthly generosity and a heart that just keeps on giving. He is the feminine energy in my life. He looks after me as much as I look after him. I've rarely had to tell him off. He's a lover not a fighter. He's the most loyal of friends. Justice and the magic of the ocean are the drivers in his life. His little kisses on my cheek are like sprinkles from heaven. We sometimes used to joke and called him the 'fun police', which is unfair as all he is doing is looking after us. Darling, I hope that you have never felt that you have had to step up and be 'Dad'. I want you to hold onto your childhood and innocence for as long as you can, but for all the times you have looked after me or told me to go and rest, I thank you.

****

My power tribe. My family of light. My Isis goddess sisters. They know me better than most and they're the ones that really get me. They see and hear the things I see, the signs, the messages, they get the downloads and the synchronicities of life. They nourish me constantly with spiritual feasts, and they keep my heart overflowing with light, my breath vibrant, and my belief strong. In fact, I cannot imagine my life without them. They are my angels (one is also the human embodiment of the Archangel Metatron and one is the incarnation of the Goddess Frejya, how awesome is that?), and they float on my angel side. My gratitude for them is abundant and ever-growing as I become more and more in touch with my spirit and my soul. Naturally, they started coming into my life around the age of 39, just when I needed them so badly. They reside all over the world, but the distance doesn't hinder our connection. If I'm honest, if all social media and modern forms of communication were to end, we would still be in touch.

One is a profound soul sister who teaches me breath, meditation and Qoya, but that's nothing compared to her teachings of resilience, perseverance, dedication and gratitude. Another teaches me the art of writing Sacred Scrolls. Another helps me access abundance, and another reminds me daily of my work to create a magical home in a mystical place by the ocean and never to give up on this dream. Another prompts me to write when I have a block, and another makes me laugh so hard, I pee my pants. The latter is also a soul who dedicated her life to caring for her elders in the most unselfish way. How she continues to joke and smile is a mystery even to me sometimes (the 'silver lining soul'), but that's her gift and I just adore every cell in her body. Another created Qoya, a movement practice that I truly love. It can transport me to many different dimensions within the space of an hour. It's like a tin opener that never fails to reveal a trove of goodies and sometimes baddies. One day I will teach it. I know this deep down. I may be a slightly bonkers doting grandma going by the name of Gaga or Babushka by then, but I WILL teach this magic.

There are many more sisters that come to me regularly with teachings, love and support. You all rock my world, and I want to thank you from the very core of my soul. I cannot write words to explain what you mean to me, what you do for me and the pure, pure love that I have for you. It's a love like no other.

Then there's my blood family. My parents are the most supportive, generous, cultured, well-read, kind people. No matter where I go, no matter what I do, they are my biggest cheerleaders and I love them for that. It's that unconditional love that I only understood once I became a mum myself. Spiritually we are of a different ilk, which fascinates me. Then one day, my Fairy Godmother suggested that as an identical twin, it was my sister who chose them, which makes perfect sense as she leads a similar grounded life to my parents, even following in the same career as them. I was just along for the ride and what an extraordinarily caring ride it is.

My twin and I were like two peas in a pod growing up, although we definitely had some different traits. 'Same, same but different' is the best way to describe us. We can reduce each other to excruciating giggles and get on each other's nerves for sure. Our lives have taken such very different paths, which have highlighted our individual characters but that bond will always be there. She is a 'super trouper' of epic proportions, who 'don't take no shit' and has a heart of burnished gold. I admire her stable family life with her adorable husband, two boys and dog. She has a solid and amazing network of friends around her in a town she adores, and I often envy her sense of contentment. I definitely got her dose of 'ants' when God was dealing out the pants!

My Nana was (and still is) the one I felt closest to spiritually. Her zest for life was like no other, and the thing I loved most about her was that she didn't judge. She was wise and understood that our existence is rarely perfect, people fuck up, but life goes on and there's no gain to being bitter and holding onto the hatred and resentment. I know I inherited this from her and it created a magical bond between us. She passed on just before her 107th birthday in the most dignified, gentle way. It was the right time. I'm sure the little singing bird in Bali was Nana checking in and maybe telling me it was time to leave (maybe not forever, though). My Poppa (who passed away almost thirty years previously) is the robin that I see all over the world, so it's funny that this is the little ditty I remember them singing to me.

Two little dicky birds sitting on a wall
One named Peter, one named Paul.
Fly away, Peter, fly away, Paul!
Come back, Peter! Come back, Paul!

A Nana holds our hand for a moment

and our hearts for a lifetime.

My Charlie's Angels are the terrific stiletto-tottering, champagne-quaffing power trio who kept me sane through the horror years. They took my side when I desperately needed allies to help me cross the divorce battlefield. They dragged me to nightclubs around the world, distracting me from my crumbling world, then later, they delighted in my 'tales of the unexpected', living vicariously through me. They wanted all the sordid details that none of my other friends dare ask, knowing all too well that I could never share with them because they are still friends with my ex (something I wholeheartedly approve of, by the way, although it doesn't make life that easy sometimes). Now and again, I really needed my girls to mock the new girlfriend, badmouth my ex with the foulest of expletives and make me try on Van Cleef & Arpels earrings in New York. They dance on my devil side and I love them with all my partying heart. I am eternally grateful to have these glamorous beauties in my life.

During the year of doom, when I was getting divorced, one of my Angels sent me a beautiful email with some quotes that I just adore. She was worried she sounded like a guru but I totally disagree. Friends need to know how impactful messages like that really are. They make all the difference on a day when you just need to find that glimmer of hope.

'Love is never lost. If not reciprocated, it will flow back and soften and purify the heart.'

– Washington Irving

'The future belongs to those who believe in the beauty of
their dreams.'

– Eleanor Roosevelt

'We must be willing to let go of the life we have planned,
so as to have the life that is waiting for us.'

– EM Forster

'When people are determined, they can
overcome anything.'

– Nelson Mandela

My 'old dependables', now that makes them sound horribly boring, which they most certainly are not. They are the solid, reliable, loyal group of guys and gals. Some I went to uni with. I lived through the baby and toddler years and beyond with some of them. Some I have simply met along the way. Always there for a cuppa, a hug and a natter. I sent my emails to them; they bought my tea and came to the lovely community events at my home. One of my favourite events was a monthly supper club called 'Love Eat Share' that I set up to bring together a motley crew of my closest girlfriends ... a journalist, a chef, a health coach, two yoga teachers, all mums and all with an extra special glow in their hearts. We shared recipes and raucous laughter, and the evenings flew by. Another extraordinary gaggle has very recently come into my life and provides me with the 'pant-wetting' laughter I desire. Adoringly known as 'The Minges' (don't ask), they remind me that deep down, I really am an English girl with a terribly inappropriate English sense of humour.

The Juicy Gang as I like to call them, are a group of girls and boys who I fell in love with whilst juicing and exercising my arse off at Jason Vale's retreat centre in Portugal (@juicemasterretreats). Who'd have thought that such an eclectic group of juice fans could bond so intently in just one week? I think it has something to do with the effect of detox and the vulnerability it brings you. They're a bundle of energy (that's the understatement of the century) and their words of encouragement and support mean the world to me. I should add that I cannot recommend Jason's place highly enough. It does exactly what it says on the tin. It's luxurious in a down to earth kind of way and after just one week there I feel like a new woman. I've been four times already but have met people who have gone there more than 40 times!

And last but not least, Chips! Three women in my life who I share absolutely everything with, and I mean everything! They know me better than a priest knows the Bible. I trust that whatever I share with them is one hundred percent confidential, and that means the world to me, to all of us, in fact. Our weekly get-togethers are therapeutic, honest, plucky and a true reflection of real life with no airs and graces, exaggerations or embellishments, just the nitty-gritty of everyday life.

I know that the people I need will come into my life when I need them and teach me the things I need to know. I trust this implicitly since the day a healer with shocking pink hair stopped on the way out of a barn in Cornwall and told me so. I was on a solo weird and wonderful raw food retreat, and she had given me some kind of mind-blowing healing treatment. Years and years later, she turned up on my terrace at a holistic garden party that I was hosting in the South of France ... go figure!

When angels sense you need them, and angels always do, they come unseen from everywhere to help and comfort you. Another angel sent to me when I needed him most was a Portuguese Vietnamese healer, who a lovely friend recommended when I was seriously scared just after my cancer diagnosis. He told me that I was going to be absolutely fine and I believed him. He flipped my whole mindset in the calmest, most understated way. That experience was a game-changer. He also said in a cool, calm voice, 'No *man* would do that,' referring to you-know-who. Those are words I will never forget.

Over the years, I have definitely become more discerning about who I spend my time with. Although I crave people's ideas and opinions, it's important to remember that everyone has their own agenda. I am choosing to create a life where I spend more time with the people who really matter to me, no matter where in the world they are and no matter how, whether it's in person, by phone, message or voicemail. Your vibe really does build your tribe, and for sure, your tribe helps to build your vibe.

'Be around people that are good for your soul.'

THE ENDING, OR IS IT
THE BEGINNING?

It's strange as I was going to start my tale with the words below, whereas now I feel it is way more appropriate to end my story (for now) with this. As the writer Mallarme said rather beautifully, 'Un livre ne commence ni ne finit; tout au plus fait-il semblant.' A translation just doesn't do it justice, but roughly, it means, 'A book neither starts nor finishes; at best it pretends to.'

'Where do I start? With the sad bit? With the happy bit? As a fictional tale or as a self-help manual? As an ironic, middle-aged look at the twists and turns of life? I feel too young to write a self-help book but too old to write a sensational tale of sexual antics.' Those were words I wrote many years ago.

So, to answer the question above, I wrote this story for myself. An unapologetic account of a part of my life that I recall with joy and sadness, smiles and tears, gratitude and hope. And why did I call my book *No Matter Where?* I have come to realise that home can be 'no matter where' as long as I am connected to my children. The unconditional love between us creates our home, and it is the only unconditional love that I have for anyone in the world. Our love is the look into each other's eyes, knowing that we're safe and held together, loose enough to move freely but tight enough not to fall. Love is the exhale when we snuggle up and I can cover them in my warm, soothing blanket of truth. Love is waking up to a new day together. Love is the ache in my belly when they're not emotionally close to me. Love is our fight to continue to adventure, our fearless hope for the future. Our love is a beautiful jewel never bought, never sold. These words were totally inspired by the beautiful song 'Home' by Imelda May. I dare you to listen.

I'm in a place I've never been before, and I'm not talking about where I'm residing! I'm talking about spiritually and mentally. Things are changing and it's utterly exciting. I'm loving the rollercoaster ride. It's not in the slightest bit scary. It's exhilarating, yet peaceful too and yes, let's be realistic here, there are a few painful contractions along the way, but as a bestie explained, 'That's just me birthing my new life.' I'm the healthiest I've ever been. I'm the juiciest

I've ever been. I love my body for the first time ever, wobbly bits and all (including those thighs). I can hold my own. I have a newfound confidence. I have an abundance of 'va va voom' and I'm loving it. I'm going to keep on exploring for a while yet. Yes, I hope with a beloved by my side. I would love a male influence in the home for my kids, and a lover and a companion for myself, and I am positive when the time is right, it will happen, as is often confirmed by the card below, which I regularly pull.

Oracle Card 34 – *Wild Kuan Yin Oracle* by Alana Fairchild

Blessings of the Khata Bestowed

In your heart, a desire for union grows, an impulse to move deeper into love's embrace. As you open your heart, I am able to gift you with my healing balm and blessing. It is never too late for love. It is never too late for joy. It is never too late for connection. As my blessing vests in your heart, a path will open up for you, leading you into love's expansive landscape. You are worthy of such blessing and shall be in the joy of its embrace.

'Fall in love with someone who is both your safe place and your biggest adventure.'

I believe that the Universe has a plan for me, that my destiny is mapped out. I also believe that I need to be in the right place to align with that destiny and the way to do this is to be my true self, to stay on that path, to not be swayed by those that do not serve me, not to be tempted by stuff that doesn't nourish me, to keep finding my True North. I need to remind myself time and time again, and as long as I do this, I will continue to live the most exciting, beautiful life.

And on that note, I shall say cheerio and the most humongous thank you from the heart of my cleansed bottom! I am overjoyed and proud to have finally finished this tale. It has been a huge gift to write and reflect and digest. It has made me stronger. It has shone a torch on my vulnerability, and above all, it has made me smile an even bigger smile than I normally have on my face, which is saying something.

I have a rather lovely feeling right now ...

You did not come here to accomplish life
Nor to be scared of it.
You came here to experience it.
Never the end
Always a new beginning ...

'Until you spread your wings,
you have no idea how far you can fly.'

Ingram Content Group UK Ltd.
Milton Keynes UK
UKHW020029220723
425570UK00011B/144